Leadership in Unknown Waters

Liminality as Threshold to the Future

Lisa R. Withrow

The Lutterworth Press

THE LUTTERWORTH PRESS

P.O. Box 60
Cambridge
CB1 2NT
United Kingdom

www.lutterworth.com
publishing@lutterworth.com

Paperback ISBN: 978 0 7188 9551 8
PDF ISBN: 978 0 7188 4808 8
ePub ISBN: 978 0 7188 4809 5
Kindle ISBN: 978 0 7188 4810 1

British Library Cataloguing in Publication Data
A record is available from the British Library

First published by The Lutterworth Press, 2020
Copyright © Lisa R. Withrow, 2020

Contents

"The ways of water"
New Zealand, 2015

Leadership in Unknown Waters

List of Illustrations

Photographs by Lisa R. Withrow

Acknowledgements

As a woman who finds great delight in adventures in natural spaces all over the globe and in my own backyard, I have known what it means to have companions and conversation partners on these journeys and the human journey. These friends know me at my deepest depths and my greatest joys; it is a gift when we hold silence together, send messages at the right time or talk and laugh until we are hoarse.

My gratitude for this book goes specifically to five of these companions, one who recently died. I especially thank Sandra Selby, an energetic travel companion to some of the most amazing places on earth and a companion-thinker who helped me generate ideas for this book and followed by offering a keen editorial eye; Bishop Karen Oliveto, a courageous and powerful leader, who gifted me space at her cottage in Nova Scotia to write while gazing out at the Atlantic, with breaks to photograph bald eagles as they regularly flew nearly within touching distance of me; Kara Jones, an encouraging, life-giving presence, who tells beautiful stories of the human spirit and who offers practical back-up with the gift of fixing broken things and loving my animals as much as I do; Blandy Taylor, a healer and wise woman, who awakened me to the reality of the collective unconscious and the power of water as a spiritual metaphor; and Jennifer Macrae (d. 2018), a spirit-grounding soul friend, who helped me see and experience liminal, "thin" spaces and adventures all over Scotland when I turned up one day as her neighbor.

I am grateful always.

A Short Introduction – Why Working in Transitional Space Matters

This book is a synthesis of my various formal and informal life-roles, all of which have brought me lessons about how I choose to live in the world. After decades of teaching and consulting, I am sure that the global concerns we face stem from a lack of courageous, emotionally intelligent leaders whose ethics call them to lead for the common good. As one voice among multitudes paying attention to the leadership field, I notice that there is not much available outside change theory/process work that addresses living well in uncertainty while using that space to create imaginative ways forward to better the planet. The wise thinkers and leaders whom I mention in this book bring their own perspectives to this crucial work, and I am grateful for their focus on meaningful leadership beyond techniques to build personal or organizational success. We live in destructive, "addicted-to-power" times, with grave consequences for the health of humanity and the planet. Local countermovements to rising narcissistic and tyrannical leadership occurring worldwide are crucial for the well-being of the planet and all who dwell here. There is urgency to develop a non-violent, effective response in the midst of an increasingly traumatized world population and planet. I don't have specific fixes, and, indeed, am suspicious of "quick fixes," having experienced firsthand the general ineffectiveness of such short-term remedies and the long-term problems they sometimes cause. I believe that our conversations and relationships foster alternatives, especially when we are intentional about meeting each other in the thresholds of uncertainty. I offer a method to evoke such alternatives in groups, teams, organizations, institutions, families and in one's own self.

My method intersects the human imagination through a visual, living metaphor (water), with attention to space (liminality, or transitional space), and focus on role (leadership development) for powerful engagement with what organizational learning theorists call "the emerging future." Here, the theoretical meets the practical, the research meets the "how to" and "why."

Like some of the authors I cite, I am clear that this method is for local participation rather than mega-problem solving on a global scale. Living in liminal space, with all its facets and challenges, is the crucible from which leaders rise as refined, rooted persons, clear about their purpose in their work and relationships. The chapters that follow invite us into the movement of the liminal, the threshold between the present and the future; I hold great hopes that a new imagination and corresponding action will arise, calling for powerful, positive change where we dwell, and making meaning of our work. to make meaning of our work that calls for powerful, positive change where we dwell.

"Rough waters"
New Zealand, 2015

Prologue

WATER

The Significance of Water as Life-Metaphor

In time and with water, everything changes.
– Leonardo da Vinci[1]

Water, in all its forms, is what carries the knowledge of life throughout the universe.
– Anthony T. Hincks[2]

Ever since I was a young child, I have paid attention to the elements around me, having an acute response to sounds, visual aesthetics and the interplay of light and dark in the world. I now realize how much my lifelong fascination with natural surroundings has shaped this approach to leadership in my more than two decades serving as an academic and a practitioner in the field of leadership studies and development. I studied environmental biology and theology stemming from this love of natural systems and the mysterious significance of the relationship of the elements to each other. Earth, fire, air, water and the organisms dependent on them, intermingle and sometimes clash with each other to create ever-evolving landscapes, in their extremes either stunningly breathtaking or devastating beyond measure.

On occasion, as I scroll through tens of thousands of nature photographs I have taken over the years, I note that most pictures focus on some aspect of water: waves, rivers, rain, glaciers, icebergs, clouds, boat wakes, landscapes punctuated by water-flows or reflections shimmering up from mirrored surfaces. I am indeed keen on this one element above the others, even as a land-dweller, though I never wish to separate it from the complexity of its life with its companion elements. Water loses its meaning and purpose without interplay with earth, fire and air, like hot springs evolving from interaction with volcanic lava, creating steam, moisture, and in large areas, whole weather systems. The cycles of the elements flow together much like liquid itself.

Strangely, water in its three primary forms exhibits the properties of all the other elements: the translucence of cloud as vapor, or invisible steam (like air), the solidity of ice (like earth) and flowing transience (like fire).[3] Water in its liquid and vapor states also does not have noticeable form of its own above the molecular level; it takes the shape of whatever contains it. At the same time, it does not dissipate unless it manifests as vapor or steam. So, while water holds together as hydrogen and oxygen, it also flows. It shows structural integrity of make-up and is agile and, at times, unpredictable. The element of water exhibits myriad paradoxes: it is both contained and free; it is both gentle and strong; it is buoyant and heavy; it covers and reflects; it has depth and breadth; it nourishes and erodes.

Water is the foundation for life because it can nurture, but it is an element almost always in flux. It has the power to give and sustain life and to carry pieces of the planet, including humanity, from here to there. It also has the power to flood and destroy in massive, turbulent strength. Lack of water also devastates all life, allowing wind to do its erosive work on the land to create desert, where very few species are able to dwell.

This substance also evokes a human response in us. As poet-writer Eila Carrico says:

> We have an innate sense that the place where land meets water is a liminal space, a space with a personality and an agenda of her own. She acts as a

gatekeeper between the surface layers of awareness and the less traversed depths of our individual psyches. It is she who chooses when and how and why to open that carefully guarded threshold. If we spend enough time at the edge of the water, she will consider this an invitation to splay open our souls, and we will eventually have to confront the unseen depths of our watery past.[4]

Two summers ago, I picked up a beautiful green and red-layered stone the size of my hand from a beach on the western Scottish island of Iona. It shone in the waves and I was enamored with its uniqueness. The waves played happily with it, and yet I was acutely aware that this stone had been shorn off its parent rock sometime not so long ago, judging from its rough edges. There were no other stones around like it in shape but there were many larger rocks with the same deep, startling color patterns, worn smooth. Somehow, this stone was brought to shore in its new and lovely form, like the other stones but, before its journey, it had "experienced" a split that seemed sudden and harsh based on the ragged gouges on its edges. The power of water to split stone and move it is much akin to Carrico's words: water can splay open not only rock but our own souls, particularly when we are confronted by pressures and changes.

In Celtic traditions, bodies of water are thought to be imbued with the qualities of healing, purification, wisdom and transformation. Rivers connect to poetic wisdom-sayings and divine inspiration. Wells or springs are associated with sacred knowledge and yet can cause harm. Whirlpools, waterfalls and sacred vessels carry prophesy and other divine qualities.[5]

In several Native American traditions, water is connected with feminine roles and symbolism:

While men would typically hunt for game, women were expected to gather water and conduct ceremonies to preserve this vital resource. Water's life force was symbolized by its rush from the mother preceding birth. Protecting the purity of springs is still a deep

spiritual responsibility felt by Sokaogon people, who
believe that surface water and groundwater represent
the lifeblood of *Nookomis oki*, or Grandmother Earth.[6]

All major world religions understand water as the medium
for purification, either before rituals or at times of great change.
Some use water as a symbol or means for rites of passage in
the faith, as in Christian baptism. Hinduism declares daily
ablutions an obligation; pilgrimage is always to a holy place
near rivers or other bodies of water, and funerals are conducted
at burial sites next to water. Judaism, Buddhism, Hinduism,
several African religions and Islam have water purifying
rituals for the body after death. Prayer traditions in Judaism
and Hinduism connect to ritual washing. Ultimately, water
has mystical implications for spiritual and religious traditions
and rituals, in addition to providing a necessary element for
life and a metaphor for life's journey.

I chose water as the metaphor signifying paradox for the
conversation in this book. We human beings live in similar
paradoxes – contained and free, gentle and strong, buoyant
and heavy, hiding and shining forth, living in our soul-
depths and at other times expansively. We are nourished or
diminished. In between the seeming contradictory states of the
paradox[7] is the "and," the fluid ability to hold two things in
one space at the same time. This flow of life cannot be denied.
In the flow, we experience thresholds where we pass over
particular points or spaces into new space and time. It is the
threshold and the in-between, or liminal, space that transitions
us forward along the connecting line of our paradoxical points.
Like water, we are always moving, transitioning from "this" to
"that." Traveling through transition, or threshold of change,
has its own challenges and it is in this liminal time and space
that the essence of water can instruct us.

Leaders Moving into Unknown Waters

In the midst of the human desire for safety and certainty,
and the fearful suspicion that often arises when that security
seems absent, this study calls for a new kind of leadership.

Human beings seem to keep seeking ultimate control of physical, emotional and spiritual concerns, affecting the state of the planet through a particularly anxious lens of ethical and moral decision-making. My hope is that my words will be in conversation with your spirit so that together we learn to live and lead differently in our spheres of influence.

I invite us into an awareness of the movements in our lives, with particular focus on the liminal, or in-between spaces, where transitions are afoot. The threshold-crossing[8] nature of liminal space creates potential for learning-adventure. In this space, to extend our water metaphor, we can ride the waves or swim deep into the depths. We encounter our need for the other elements (air, solid ground, heat) while we are buoyed by water's nurture. We "intersect" with our own bodies and elements that are not part of us, though we carry water inside of us.[9] Water flows through us and also carries our beings to new places. Paradoxically, we retain who we are while we change at the same time.

How we learn to flow is critical for formation and maturing into flourishing. This book itself moves through liminal space, starting at equilibrium (where we start), moving to threshold space (liminality) to a new home (future equilibrium). Part I explores why attending to liminal space matters for experiencing meaningful transition. Discussion about starting the journey and creating openness to the entry of threshold space follows. We begin the separation from the familiar and move into middle space. Each chapter in Part II covers a facet of water as metaphor, namely, as a way to imagine being and leading in liminal space as we traverse the moving waters of transition. Part III brings us home with transformed understandings of ourselves in relation to others, incorporating us in new ways in previous contexts.

My intent is to focus on persons who are in leadership roles in a variety of capacities and contexts, calling them to create awareness through their own journeys so that they might invite others into similar space. Leaders who do not do this awareness work are disingenuous if they wish to evoke such work in others. Therefore, there are two purposes that can be utilized here: immersion for leaders attending to transitional spaces; and subsequent invitation for those whom they lead to enter these spaces for the purpose of powerful, positive change in one's place of work and in relational connections. Inviting groups of people into liminal work invites them into a particular kind of innovative and transformative space for agile, creative movement in business, social, and religious enterprises.

This book invites you to enter liminal space by crossing from certainty into a threshold of adventure as a way to experience transitions toward richer relationships, higher awareness, expansive productivity, deeper meanings, greater resilience and intersections yet undiscovered. Its purpose is to counter the polarization that is now the norm in our world with development of a third way of leading and living that embraces paradox for the benefit of relationships, well-being and greater freedom.

Unlike many books on group dynamics and conflict, this is not a book of checklists designed for a quick fix. I presume that journeys into the liminal are not prescribed with outcomes based on skill sets alone. My intention in these chapters is to create a "container" for meaningful work that good leader-facilitators can take and use for their own purposes and in their own fashions. The work is based on dialogue and intentional participation in liminal space, with water as our guiding metaphor, pointing to creating a greater good for our work and our societies.

As we begin, poet David Whyte invites us into the water:[10]

Where Many Rivers Meet

All the water below me came from above.
All the clouds living in the mountains
gave it to the rivers,
who gave it to the sea, which was their
dying.

And so I float on cloud become water,
central sea surrounded by white mountains,
the water salt, once fresh,

cloud fall and steam rush, tree roots and
tide bank,
leading to the rivers' mouths
and the mouths of the rivers sing into the
sea,
the stories buried in the mountains
give out into the sea
and the sea remembers
and sings back,
from the depths,
where nothing is forgotten.

Part I

LEADING INTO UNKNOWN WATERS

In this part of the journey, we will discuss what liminality is and why time spent in intentional liminal space is important for leaders and their teams who seek to move forward into an innovative future. This intentionality is especially important in the midst of pandemic health crises, wars, and financial hardship experienced at local and global levels. Initial crossing into in-between or transitional space has particular preconditions that make the work meaningful. A skilled facilitator is necessary to create a "container" or a holding space for the conversations. These conversations, which often will include vision-work, attention to next steps, writings and silences, eventually emerge from a deeper consciousness and, ideally, the "collective unconscious." Setting some parameters around the flow of thinking and creativity keeps liminal space navigable rather than opening up complete chaos in the process.

"Passages"
Antarctica, 2007

Chapter One

Why Liminal Space Matters for Leaders

Water has the kind of mutability that makes it such a hospitable metaphor for change. Water can inhabit the offered shape and yet keep to itself. It has the power of metamorphosis.
– John O'Donohue[1]

Water is an apt symbol for the flow of life. It moves within and through our bodies as a dominant element and throughout our landscapes in its various forms. Water variously moves freely within its contained space, permeates and floods and freezes, holding everything still or blocking the way. Sometimes water vaporizes and dissipates into the air, still moving freely but no longer contained or visible at all.

The nature of water itself in its manifested forms is to move. Even the seemingly immobile quality of ice is ever-challenged to change and move by pressure, temperature, and dehydration unless it exists in a vacuum. In its movement, water carries life and substance from one place to another; we can see the debris trapped in the ice of glaciers as they move downhill. Water crosses a whole variety of thresholds and journeys on, finding its way to the sea and to the sky to be recycled back into another flow once again. Its liminality as an element surpasses all the other elements because water can move in many forms and under almost any conditions.

Such is the way with our living. There are moments where we flow from one encounter, situation or relationship to the next. Life is adventuresome. Then there are times when we need to stand stalwart and clear about our stances and intentions. Life is conflicted, disruptive, or trauma-inducing. And there are times when we simply let things go because we no longer control or even desire to control them. Life is freeing.

There is also possibility for water to be contained in unnatural ways, such as through human constructs like dams, fountains, human-made spillways, swimming pools or retaining pools. While this fluid element moves in each of these containers, it is controlled for purposes of reservoir, flood prevention, decoration or recreation. Ice and steam also can be used, respectively, to preserve and to cleanse; each contained phase of the element provides a tool for intended life-improvement.

In addition to these movements and uses of water, we know also that water can become so polluted or silted that it is a danger both to life within and around it. News stories from all over the world speak of water contamination and there are some theories that there is no longer any purely clean water on earth. Likewise, our own life-flows can become "stuck" in torpor, disease, unhealthy models and subconscious destructive tendencies, blocking us from health and well-being. The flourishing of life around us and within us wanes as the poisons build up to toxic levels. In time, we become accustomed to the lack of clear flow, shining ice or freeing vapor. We pay attention to our emergencies and our concerns, pushing our attention to the immediate rather than the flow. The call for innovative, forward-thinking leaders today is to counter any blockage by invoking a journey into a third space where we learn anew what the flow of life and leadership means. This third space exists in the transition times and places; it is a threshold called "liminal space." From it arises creative thinking, evoking a different or "third way" forward when decision-making or choices have become entrenched in binary "either/or." Third ways are essential for eliminating polarization and moving into the "and" of paradox, the win-win, in our so-called "VUCA" (Volatile, Uncertain, Complex, Ambiguous) era.[2] Indeed, at this writing in spring 2020, the VUCA world is clearly upon us all as the globe battles the novel coronavirus with health crises, equipment shortages, quarantines, travel restrictions, business closures, and rising unemployment. This third space has been a surprise for most of the world, and the responses have varied greatly, including deep polarization. Some leaders have resorted to command-and-control, and some have decided to wait until the virus takes its course. Many are practicing a Third Way: functioning watchfully and responding daily to new data while trying to grasp what the unknown future might bring. In time, we will see a new kind of world in terms of relationships and financial intersections, but for now, we are in deep liminal space.

What Is Liminality?

In order to appreciate the importance of liminality to the challenges facing twenty-first-century leaders, a brief description of the concept of "liminal space" as it has been developed in anthropology and the study of ecosystems will be helpful. The word "liminal" originates from the Latin "limen," which means "threshold."[3] One can think of thresholds as transition spaces between one place and another – for example, the threshold of a door frame from one room to another, or the bank between the land and the flowing river water, or a bridge across a deep canyon. Liminality is "neither this nor that" or "both this and that."[4]

Crossing into the threshold is moving into transition space. This space also involves the temporal; it is not meant for permanent dwelling. If one stays on or in the threshold forever, one is caught between two places, and completion of the transition, called "incorporation," or new equilibrium, does not occur. The view ahead may be expansive in threshold space but movement toward what is next stops if one does not find mobilization and momentum to work toward it.

Therefore, while liminality is most often described as space, time is a factor in the liminal as well. Ethnographers give us a human-focused view of this kind of space-time.

"Liminal" is a word first used in this context by ethnographer Arnold van Gennep in the nineteenth century, based on his studies of tribal rites of passage in Australia and Africa.[5] In his work, he studied how rhythms of collective life developed a ritualized pattern or process by which people made meaning of life's progression. For example, van Gennep observed the change of status for males in a tribe as a highly ritualized transition via threshold/liminal space when boys reached a particular age. To become men – or in other words, to secure a status change within the tribe – they had to enter a transitional phase that tested their abilities and strength. Boys were sent from their villages into the wilderness, separated from all they knew, often for a number of weeks. They were left without companions and without life-sustaining food and water, expected to find their way by surviving in their wilderness. If they did survive, after a certain period of time, they were allowed to move back into the tribe, reunited and reincorporated into its life but as men with new identities and roles.

As van Gennep observed, the three phases of this journey include moving into a threshold, or liminal space, over a boundary or border (separation that moves one into threshold), living in the wilderness (transition within threshold where awareness-raising and testing occurs) and then returning, albeit with new identity and a new sense of home (incorporation that moves one back into the community).[6] The middle phase, transition, is the liminal space. In it, events happen and decisions are made that are based on our beliefs, ethics, instincts and learned behavior but, at the same time, we are in unknown territory and the flow of life may not make much sense; the behavior that has worked for us thus far is no longer entirely helpful in our current context. Unusual occurrences are likely to manifest themselves in this liminal space: new thoughts, dramatic insights, changing values, loss, life lived with discomfort and perhaps physical and emotional threat, ability to take more risks, new meaning for life or work and a focus on what comes next, even if that next phase is not yet clear.

Interestingly, van Gennep and his later followers (including Victor Turner, a twentieth-century anthropologist) claimed that life and the development of culture are not possible without liminal spaces and times at both personal and social levels. Transition is built into the progression of life, whether social or organizational.

Another way to understand liminal space in terms of environmental systems rather than human systems is to think about the nature of ecotones.[7] An "ecotone" is the transitional area between two stable ecological systems. For example, there are shorelines with dunes, beaches, rocks, or other embankments where water and land meet, and where species of both ecologies live and overlap. Yet, there are also unique habitats in the overlapping area. Usually, this space is biologically diverse. Birds and fish exist together, as do turtles, frogs and crustaceans. Various sea grasses or freshwater reeds grow in the ecotone. This space also has a natural tension to it, hence the "tone" of "ecotone" (Greek for "tension"). Therefore, this transitional space is fragile, vulnerable and always evolving. At the same time, the richness of this space stems from its diversity of life and its resilience.

Thus, the tension, while consistent with the riskiness of the habitat, also provides opportunity in the midst of its inherent complexity. Animals and plants adapt to in-between space, able to function on the edges of two different "homes." For example, sea turtles, puffins and other animals lay their eggs in burrows on the land and live most of their lives sustaining themselves at sea. Their offspring upon birth must learn to navigate the middle space to survive, launching from land to water, then back again to further the species when they reproduce. This ecotone is essential for the balance of species throughout the planet.

Think too of a forest and a meadow. The space between them has small trees and meadow grasses. It also has plants and animals that exist only in that particular middle zone, the ecotone or liminal space. As the forest advances and the trees grow, the zone evolves and moves outward until it encounters a mountain. Then the forest adjusts again to rocky terrain; the trees may not have the level of nourishment they had in the meadow areas, so they don't grow as tall. The winds may be harsher, so trees focus on breadth of root systems, surviving better in sheltered areas. Animals in one zone advance with the vegetation until they are unable to survive a particular climate. This danger and subsequent adaptation do not stop the growth of trees or animals, they simply create transitional growing conditions for the trees and animals until they can incorporate into new spaces by adapting for their own survival.

Ecotones, or liminal spaces, sometimes take on spiritual significance. In ancient times, the concept of space was very important for rituals. For example, the Celts connected particular spaces, which they called "thin places," with the liminal transition between the physical world and the spiritual world. They noted that there were particular geographies or boundaries that were thin veils between daily life and experience of the soul-world. Margaret Silf, who writes about spiritual practices, speaks of thin places as those where the visible world meets the invisible world, the world of mystery. Furthermore, liminal space is not always physical; it can be an internal state of being. Silf names transitions that human beings encounter in this liminality: beginning at birth, discovering our surroundings in childhood, questing for inner truth as we grow, setting out into new ventures, turning and returning when we lose our way, seeking companionship for belonging, encountering transition times and boundary seasons when we experience life beyond our imagination.[8]

Those who commit to spiritual practices find that these transitions are occasions for rites of passage or ritual, much as van Gennep found in his study of tribal customs. Thin places, like ecotones and ritualized status changes in life's transitions, become spaces of change and growth, even if there is danger involved.

Thin places in Celtic life also have a time component attached to them in the cycles of transition. For example, rituals accompany natural annual occurrences such as the equinoxes and the solstices. In religious traditions across the globe, there are cyclical rituals that are based on the calendar or timing of natural phenomena. Space and time connect, weaving together a larger sense of "liminal space."[9]

Why Liminality?

Liminality is inevitable. There are life-passages, such as adolescence, a not-quite-child and not-quite-adult status which yet holds characteristics of both levels of maturity. There are places like airports or stairwells that provide movement from a starting point to a destination without intention of dwelling in waiting areas or between floors forever (unless the flights are canceled or doors are locked, of course!). Weddings, deaths, births, divorces, all are liminal in that they require a shift from one state of being to another, in some cases, via ritual and, in some, via emotional processes such as grief. Change in professional roles, job shifts or product-market disruptions also create transitional space, which requires learning new ways of thinking and setting alternative goals.

Because liminality is a part of life at every stage, and because transition is built into our ecosystems, our own life-development and organizational advancement, it makes sense to attend to it intentionally. Those who are counselors, chief executive officers, decision-makers, artists, medical careworkers, shamans, teachers, spiritual directors, midwives, writers, leaders of rituals, storytellers or entertainers, to name a few, all engage in liminal work regularly. People who are in the midst of moving homes or changing jobs experience liminal time and space because they are living with transition. So, liminality is nothing new.

However, what has been neglected in the development of leaders is the intentional work to learn how to immerse into the liminal, either with a group or a team or as a solo traveler. To do so is to set a direction that willingly crosses a boundary from "what we have always done," repeating formulas that presume ongoing success, ultimately leading to a blockage or even failure. Instead, entering into intentional dislocation and disruption for a period of time for the sake of deeper formation as a leader or a team opens people to the risk of uncertainty, while also yielding transformative perspectives and Third Way mobilization for life and work. Such perspectives may not be possible if one does not enter into a new kind of flow that moves from the old way of being to a new way of seeing the world and one's meaningful leadership role within it.

The task before us is to know that liminal space, created intentionally or unintentionally, with particular border-crossings and boundaries, is an essential space for the evolution of excellent leadership and, indeed, meaningful life. It is not meant to be a place or time for problem-solving, but for a sojourn into the unknown that contains within it both the characteristics of one's starting point and a hoped-for future, much like an ecotone or a passage into adulthood. Liminal space is an interval of possibility that invites transition. This space, while characterized by flow, is also "contained."

There is a time-component involved when one enters this experience; endings and beginnings are essential markers for separation from familiar habits and thoughts. Between those endings and beginnings lies the transition that leads to incorporation in a new way, status or role. The ending of the old way and the beginning of the new occurs when one arrives at what might be called a new home. Furthermore, boundary-crossing into the liminal occurs multiple times in the course of a lifetime – there are *many* points along the flow of life where a person or team will have transition times, then move into the "new" meaning and purpose, until the next threshold reveals itself.

As van Gennep and Turner, among others, claimed: without transition, there is no growth. So, for leaders and their teams, as well as individuals, creating intentional transitional experience necessitates space where formational development occurs. This approach moves more powerfully and sustainably toward change than continuing education seminars required by organizations. It also is preferable to formal education with a set curriculum and predetermined outcomes, which assume that transition can be codified for assessment purposes in a very particular way. Predetermined desired outcomes assume that solutions are already designated and students have to meet them rather than create their own ways of thinking and choices about how to be leaders in the world. Creating liminal space also is a powerful, positive alternative to business leadership literature that concentrates on checklists for skill-set development, assessments or surveys of leadership characteristics that are most likely to raise profits or create new markets. All of these components of leadership education may connect with the liminal experience, but they do not allow for imaginative, substantive responses to the call for change. Much like the banks of a river contain and affect the flow of water, they do not define the water itself, nor what it carries, nor ultimately its rate of flow at all times.

Many conditions affect the changing contexts of leadership, sometimes as frequently as minute by minute. To continue developing skills is required for survival and growth but to develop resilience through competent, open-minded navigation of unknown waters is lifesaving and even transformative for a person or organization. Ultimately, when leaders sense or observe the time for transition, their immersion in liminal space with their teams or companions opens the door for deep, powerful awareness and subsequent scenario-building for the emerging future.

Leadership and Liminality

Why do leaders, in particular, need to know how to dwell in liminal space when that time comes? Moreover, why would leaders want followers or other leaders to dwell there as well for a time?

Like water, information in our day and age flows into every available crevice. Information connectivity is the greatest technological power that we know in the twenty-first century. Think of the mobile phone. The minute your phone is allowed to access your location, it sends that information to thousands of other users to determine how long it will take you to drive from home to work and back again, based on traffic patterns and all the others using their GPS systems. Bank transfers and investment choices occur instantaneously around the globe. "Google" a question or ask an electronic "helper," and you have an answer within seconds. Not only does the answer come forth immediately, Google, Bing and other powerful search engines, *learn* and track your question, so that they can then send you more information, even information you may not want, through your electronic networking channels. Medical devices feed information back to doctors instantaneously so that every breath or heartbeat can be monitored while people get on with their lives. Hacking into social network accounts has potential to change election results. Only an elite few who know the intricate inner workings of communication technology understand the complexity of information flow.[10]

Connectivity also occurs through alliances beyond borders for economic infrastructures, exchange of resources, travel, medical care, and intercultural conversation.[11] Information transfer and other modes of connectivity permeate the globe and, frankly, borderless connection is now running almost all societies. In fact, one might wonder if we are all living in our own global liminal space, where the speed of learning and communication moves so fast that we never land anywhere at all. Hence, the need arises for an accompanying counterbalance to this compressed time and frenetic pace that we have developed through our electronic communication age, where we slow down to create awareness in the midst of multiple transitions occurring simultaneously. Indeed, there are times when we are forced to a standstill to become deeply aware of what is happening around us, as we witnessed in the 2020 global coronavirus (COVID-19) pandemic. Looking to tribes and cultural groups who continue to practice rituals and rites of passage becomes a relevant part of the discussion for leadership. These groups have a rooted history of creating and containing spaces for transition that have meaning and forethought, with a desired progression in experience and growth. To lose such a human connection would result in such extreme individualism that humanity will have deeper relationships with electronic devices than with the person in the same room. I hear this claim stated often by grandparents who see their grandchildren spending inordinate time on e-devices.

Therefore, creating intentional liminal space, in which human beings participate with each other in learning postures that are not prescribed or dictated by foregone expectations of outcome, is an urgent endeavor for our survival on many levels: as human beings, local businesses, societies, transnational corporations and nation-states. Ironically and paradoxically, this urgency requires slowing down. Indeed, creating intentional liminal space for the sake of a new kind of leadership development requires wise facilitators who hold space for others to enter willingly, for a particular purpose and for slowing life's pace. That purpose is initially to de-polarize persons from each other and from the earth, then introduce human connectivity in the midst of diversity; in other words, liminal space is where we are capable of learning to practice radical relatedness in times when polarization and extremism, and sometimes panic, is on the rise. We "unlearn" the propensity to react swiftly in perceived self-defense based on fear or self-righteous anger, or the need to be correct. Then we can learn or re-learn encountering each other at deeper levels. Risk and creative sustainability, a powerful paradox, hold hands in this space, affecting relationships, the purpose of work and a vision for the future. Leaders would do well to take note.

There exists a romanticized notion of what good leadership is. This view is perpetuated in the literature written by business leaders with a long list of success over the decades that suggests what a benevolent leader looks like, complete with a description of the tyrannical characteristics one must avoid. Servant-leadership, adaptive leadership, collaborative leadership, enabling leadership, all fit into this category of the best way to be a leader. However, what is at stake here is not the formula for teaching leaders how to be leaders, but the very process and experience that shapes leaders into becoming what is already within them in the context of community, be it workplace ecologies or geographical locations or even families. True, the aforementioned characteristics of agility and collaboration may be present in a leader already; but a focus on characteristics, rather than ongoing formation through relationship development, ironically creates leaders who can become static or stuck in their own work and development, often with polarized ideas about what works, what is right, who is important and unimportant, who is the enemy or competition, and what kind of authority should command situations.

Leaders who come from all walks of life have to play myriad roles in their organizations, whether they work in Fortune 500 companies, health care emergency response, not-for-profit organizations, religious bodies, political movements, or volunteer networks. If desperate situations demand quick response, then an authoritarian style may temporarily be appropriate. If internal relations are foundering, then collaborative methods make sense. If customers and stakeholders are not responsive, then persuasive tactics need to come into play. If bullies are trying to intimidate leaders, then avoidance or confrontation may be wise. If there is a large justice issue or profit at stake, then the leader must negotiate or even command steps forward.

Ultimately though, these leadership styles and the accompanying characteristics held by those with decision-making powers work long-term only if relationship connections are in a healthy space. Healthy space occurs when attention is paid to networks of people who exhibit diversity and difference – within groups and among customers or clients. Creating liminal space – space that attends to creative conversation while suspending status – leads to deeper understanding of others' values, freer exchange of ideas and a sense of risk that is shared and, therefore, paradoxically, less risky among participants. Scenarios for the future can be built in liminal space, where people and resources are used with the best thinking and deepest wisdom emerging out of the commitment to live together in-between old certainties and new possibilities, in a strong relational field.

In liminal space, liminal thinking occurs. Storytelling is the best way to ascertain the belief-systems and values that people bring to the space. Liminal thinking requires that participants step outside their own "bubbles" of belief so that they can hear others' either complementary or opposing values. This openness is what makes liminal space risky. It may mean a shift in one's worldview about how behavior, actions, or decisions "should" be chosen. Author and strategic design consultant Dave Gray says this: "Liminal thinking is the art of creating change by understanding, shaping, and reframing beliefs."[12] He goes on to say that beliefs are essential to our survival because they are tools for navigating the world through our actions. "But they also limit us. In fact, the words *liminal* and *limit* are linked; they share the same Latin root. The same boundaries that make it possible for us to think also limit what we can conceive."[13] Waking up to limiting beliefs opens us to new possibilities as we walk into new spaces of thinking and belief. This heightened awareness is essential for a third, powerful, positive way forward to allow a "win-win" situation to emerge.

Margaret Wheatley, co-founder of the Berkana Institute and long-time student of systems organization and organic development for leaders and organizations, calls for leaders to invoke people's sense of goodwill, generosity and desire for community. Her analysis of why the world is following a path to destruction helps us determine what is so important about finding and, if not finding, creating liminal space now more than ever before.[14] She claims that whole social and political belief systems and practices must collapse and become chaotic before we move into space that is healthier for everyone:

> Everything that is held together – its beliefs, meanings, and structures – no longer work now that the environment has changed. And so, the system falls apart. It descends into chaos and finally reaches a bifurcation point, where it has two choices: Either it can reorganize using new beliefs and structures that work well in the changed environment. Or it can insist on the old ways, fail to reorganize itself, and die. Both rebirth and death are possible as an outcome of the passage through chaos.[15]

Wheatley is clear that we cannot move into more life-affirming relationships and interactions without this chaotic space, which I call liminal space. She demonstrates that everything has a beginning, a middle, and an end in her survey of civilizations in *Who Do We Choose to Be?* Her aim is to find ways back to behaving sanely, with compassion and generosity, for the sake of each other and the planet. The chaotic time is, for her:

> a bitter pill for activists and all people with discerning, open hearts. We understand the complexity of the global problems, we have thought systemically to

define root causes, we have proposed meaningful
solutions, but we are impotent to influence those in
power who ignore our efforts. The powerful always
defend the status quo, because it is the source of their
power and privilege. Any change that benefits others
would destroy their position.[16]

Wheatley calls for "islands of sanity," where leaders "use
their power and influence, their insight and compassion,
to lead people back to an understanding of who we are as
human beings, to create the conditions for our basic human
qualities of generosity, contribution, community, and love to
be evoked no matter what."[17] She faces the reality of our era
and challenges leaders to choose who they wish to be in these
chaotic times, inviting them and their followers to shift away
from anxious command-and-control reactions to breakdowns
and instead, to move toward sane, thoughtful ways of being in
the world. Indeed, traversing liminal space with minds wide
open is essential for leaders in order to develop their Third
Ways that not only bring new successes to their organizations,
but also make positive impacts on the planet.

A Survey Honoring Change-Theory Thinkers and Social Scientists

Everything has a beginning, a middle and an end and then a
new beginning again: the cycle repeats itself as we see in our
metaphorical water-journey. These cycles occur more than once
as microcycles in our own lifecycles and they certainly occur
throughout macrocycles of recorded history. Civilizations
rise, peak and fall. Beings are born, transition through phases
and die. Organizations become successful, then suddenly are
no longer on the cutting edge of manufacturing, technology
or retail. Viruses rise, then fade, then a new viral strain rises
again. Such is the nature of movement through time.

As we acknowledge the cycles, we also acknowledge how we
continue to think through how to manage them well and, rather
than experiencing demise from them, we learn what lies next
on the horizon. Change-theorists, psychologists and "futuring"
thinkers have all taken on the analysis of change in the last 120

years. Most describe the cycles of change, which are important to the work here. Middle space, the transitional or liminal space, is accounted for in their work, though not as the most significant part of the passage through transition.[18] William Bridges calls this middle space the "neutral zone," where the most important work of transition occurs. "It is where the critical psychological realignments and repatternings take place. It is the very core of the transition process."[19] Below is a representation of thinkers from different disciplinary fields of focus who have paved the way for understanding change processes.

In the twentieth century, group work as a means for personal and professional support or advancement came into fashion as psychologists and others developed behavioral and organizational models of change. People were gathered for a variety of purposes, with variations on this theme continuing today. Groups could be focused on tasks, beta-testing, topical discussion, development, creative endeavors, advising, therapeutic analysis, support, advocacy, reading, behavior or self-help. Facilitating group dynamics is important in each of these kinds of groups. If facilitated well, there will be room for intentionally temporal liminal space in the midst of the group's work.

However, these aforementioned groups often focus either on a particular outcome or a therapeutic change that addresses an identified problem, rather than allowing the space itself to have its own momentum or flow. Liminal space, where diverse persons are gathered, focuses on belief systems and ethics in an adventure into unknown territory for the sake of deepening and widening one's worldview without a set outcome. This liminality allows for scenario-building and intense focus on what is appearing on the horizon but does not prematurely prescribe a remedy or plan of action. Therapeutic techniques to diagnose, treat or cure a problem or condition look backward into history. By contrast, business group-dynamic methods usually focus on the future with a particular outcome in mind.

Furthermore, intentionally temporal liminal space can be appropriated or might be endorsed, sometimes problematically, for a lifetime focus, such as recovery groups like Alcoholics Anonymous might. Entry into liminal space is more like Quaker "clearness committees"[20] or Gestalt approaches to self-discovery, engaging in co-inquiry and attention to the here and now, rather than therapy or project groups. In intentional threshold journeying, participants do not come with preconceived ideas about what might happen or to rehearse their pasts. The intent is to create a transition that *can* involve identity shift from one place to another, albeit with attention to what we already know or intuit, as one enters into and stabilizes within a new reality.

Liminal space also can be found in change-theory processes created for business development, in business schools or in change-theory developers' models that focus on what they call "emerging futures." In change theory, there is a time when all seems like chaos before something new emerges. During the chaotic time, people make decisions about whether they will invest in the work to move through the chaos into a new order, become stuck in the chaos or walk away.

Take for example, organizational development expert Kurt Lewin, a twentieth-century German-American psychologist who developed theories of organizational change and who created a change management model in 1943, much akin to force-field analysis in physics. He identified organizational tendencies to remain in a static state (security and control) when change was necessary to address evolving markets. This static state, often highly defended in order to keep it intact, is the initial point of entry to "unfreeze" a system. To do so requires an intervention or a crisis (or perceived crisis): a disruption. Then, difficult as it may be, the organization moves into immersive change – a time and space of intense learning, or liminal space, which can take quite a bit of time and effort to navigate. Finally, Lewin claims that the organization needs to "refreeze" or reinforce the change and anchor it until the next need for change comes along.[21]

Lewin's theory, though somewhat mechanistic, has also been adopted by psychologists for personal and group internal emotional and mental work. Interestingly, this process sounds significantly like van Gennep's process for rites of passage: separation from the norm, transition and incorporation or reintegration. The "change" or "transition" phase is required for life, whether in relationships or organizations, to evolve. This liminal space, then, is all-important for any kind of growth.

Another rendition of change theory based on an curve graphic can be found in an analysis of the evolution of religious organizations. Gil Rendle, who works with religious organizations, takes change processes and describes the "rollercoaster" that moves congregations from sameness to difference, often through the onset of crisis or disruption. The rollercoaster starts with the disruption at the top, then plummets through a series of possible emotional responses and subsequent actions in this liminal time, similar to the grief process, until one reaches the bottom of the valley. At that point, people have a choice: they can continue to work through the process of change or they may leave. Those who stay begin the climb up the hill on the other side of the rollercoaster, creating new vision and narratives for themselves and their work.[22] My attention here is in the space near or at the bottom of the rollercoaster, when critical participation decisions are made, including ascertaining the nature of participation in the "new" work or how reintegration into the system will occur.

Otto Scharmer, a lecturer at Massachusetts Institute of Technology, has long been interested in how we pay attention to the world based on our interior condition, from which our intentions, attention and actions originate.[23] His interests delve into the relational bridges among various groups and how traversing these bridges changes us. The dedication in his later, shorter version of Theory U is telling: "To the emerging movement of people who bridge the three major divides of our time: the ecological, the social, and the spiritual divide."[24] The word "bridge" is an operative verb for liminal work. Scharmer's approach blends systems thinking, leading change and innovation as human beings work toward a higher consciousness.[25]

Relationship-building, for Scharmer, is co-creative rather than reactive and he invites us to think about this work intentionally as groups think about emerging possibilities. He claims that leadership abilities must include the following for this kind of learning: the suspension of judgment and understanding about the world beyond our preconceived thoughts and ideas; co-sensing through connections that have potential to be seeds of the future, focusing on the power of intention (rather than corporate indoctrination), by increasing one's sources of curiosity, compassion and courage; co-creating in small ways; and container-building by building new holding spaces that activate generativity.[26] While Scharmer's Theory U needs significant explanation, its components are clear. Movement through liminal space is not merely free-flow, it is difficult, immersive work best shared within defined parameters acceptable to all involved in the conversation.

Change theory gives us a helpful insight into the process of transition. The liminal space in the progression is a particular danger zone where transition times and in-between spaces invite the most vulnerability, becoming the most difficult to navigate in any schema of change. Traversing these spaces well is essential for the formation of the next generation of leaders. As a result, as leaders engage the *need* to pay attention to liminal spaces, they have opportunity to refocus on a new horizon, evolving their organizations in depth and breadth of thinking and experience. The same is true of relationships, worker interactions, and changes in ecosystems. Energy follows intention, so for those who wish to move forward in creative and meaningful ways, we must enter this space willingly, curiously, courageously, and vulnerably. According to these thought-leaders who address change, we must create authentic space for others to risk doing the same.

Social scientist Brené Brown focuses on this mindset in her own work. Brown engages the need for quality relationships in a polarizing world by evoking personal courage to open oneself vulnerably to difference and diversity, much like Dave Gray in *Liminal Thinking*. Vulnerability and strength of self-identity combined with openness to others are essential ingredients for belonging to authentic community, and, furthermore, for being a good leader. She says this about leadership in her publication, *Dare to Lead*:

> If we want people to show up, to bring their whole selves including their unarmored, whole hearts – so that we can innovate, solve problems, and serve people – we have to be vigilant about creating a culture

in which people feel safe, seen, heard, and respected. Daring leaders must care for and be connected to the people they lead.[27]

Finding the right mindset for such work is crucial. Brown, in her earlier work, *Braving the Wilderness*,[28] discusses the importance of what she calls "wilderness" to find oneself on the courageous journey to "true belonging," a relational stance required for healing deep divisions. Her description of wilderness, a component to find "true belonging," sounds much like liminal space, though for Brown, this journey is initially a private one rather than one ritualized in community as in van Gennep's study or with a community "container" (discussed in Chapter Three), as proposed in this book.

> Theologians, writers, poets, and musicians have always used the wilderness as a metaphor, to represent everything from a vast and dangerous environment where we are forced to navigate difficult trials to a refuge of nature and beauty where we seek space for contemplation. What all wilderness metaphors have in common are the notions of solitude, vulnerability, and an emotional, spiritual, or physical quest.[29]

Transitional spaces and times are upon us all; this condition is nothing new. What is essential in a highly politicized, polarized and fast-paced world is that we navigate the liminality well, so that, like water, we flow where there is need, minimizing destruction as best we can in the service of a planet that desperately needs a new, compassionate, positive outlook to survive – and, indeed, thrive. It is time to cross into the threshold of liminal space and discover what can happen there.

"Through the gap"
Antarctica, 2007

Chapter Two

Crossing into Threshold

A good traveler has no fixed plans and is not intent upon arriving. A good artist lets his [sic] intuition lead him wherever it wants. A good scientist has freed himself of concepts and keeps his mind open to what is.
– Lao Tzu[1]

For leaders who wish to change the way we interact with one another in our work, with families, among friends, in places of worship or simply while dwelling in our neighborhoods, there is necessary work to be done in reacquainting ourselves with the nature of relationship. Our contexts differ minute-by-minute, within the workplace and then from work to home. They also differ among us depending on our geographical locations, the time of year, our cultures, belief systems and our status. We hold in common the world around us, one that seems determined to consume and compete, inviting us into these frays in our interactions throughout the day. The call here is for a learning posture, a journey to sound mind, grounded intention and relational spirit. To find our way to living in centered and focused ways is to enter into the work of opening ourselves to new possibilities of thinking and experiencing. This intentionality requires entering new space voluntarily so that we can change the trajectory of the world around us as we change ourselves. We claim self-agency as we move into risk and uncertainty with others, knowing that we will change and perhaps be transformed individually and together by role or by values held, but still remain centered in our own identities as worthy human beings.

The water metaphor helps. When it is time to move from the land of solid footing where we are most comfortable into liminal space, we notice that we are surrounded by challenges and ideas that exhibit properties like water. In other words, we move from a beginning or starting point, equilibrium, our *status quo*, to the middle – transition space and time. Swimmers walk or dive in, and boaters launch. We enter the water. Swimmers know that water buoys and holds us in our movement. Boaters understand this buoyancy and stabilizing ballast. Others simply wade in as far as they can without "going under."

Water is not the human being's natural, permanent dwelling place. We who encounter immersion into water understand its properties enough to know that it can carry us, hold us, ease our muscle pain or even overcome us with strong currents, low temperatures, raging floods or antagonistic creatures who dwell there. Diving into the water or even walking in gingerly to "get used to it" holds both promise and risk.

Thus, we begin our crossing into the middle space of transition. We have established that liminal space is an experiential process in which we must dwell for a time so that we move from our current understanding of existence in our workplace and our life-space to form a new, heightened awareness. We have potential to develop more context-appropriate views as the world changes rapidly around us, especially when we are forced into an unexpected crisis. To do this work, we move into the threshold, which is liminal space. We walk into the threshold, we immerse in the water. Why do we move into the water? Sometimes we are forced by circumstance to move into transition – a job change, family changes, birth or death, an accident, dissatisfaction, or a disaster. Sometimes we simply know that the current state of being isn't enough or is no longer relevant because we have outgrown it or been thrust into new circumstances and so we make an intentional choice for change.

To move into transition, into the threshold where we are in-between, not quite "this" or "that" and, at the same time, a bit of both "this" and "that," means that we will encounter disruption to our normalcy. The intent to move into such space deliberately will require an accompanying willingness to release particular ways of functioning, belief systems and even methods of thinking and acting. A great deal can happen in the liminal space, should we be flexible and agile enough to swim in its currents and follow its path rather than panicking and trying to retain control. The following possibilities are encounters that might occur when entering liminal space.

Suspending belief systems and long-held conclusions is a component of entering the water. Unlearning habits of thought and practice are necessary as well. What works while moving on dry land does not work the same way when traveling in water. To move into threshold space means to open one's mind expectantly for surprises and perhaps discomfort. When the work is deep enough, there may be a refining quality to it – what is unnecessary is shed. Existing in water is also tiring. We have to keep afloat while experiencing the sensations surrounding us and keeping an eye open for danger: swift currents, rocks, unfriendly beasts and change in flow or temperature. At first, no matter what our hopes are for transformative experience, we simply attend to survival and then learn to sustain ourselves in alien space. We don't know what will happen and such uncertainty often leads to swimming for safety or pushing against any hint of danger. Sometimes the discomfort or disruption leads us to thrash about or lash out, endangering everyone. So, knowing what is possible as we cross into threshold space can steady us for the journey.

Over two decades ago, I conducted research in Great Britain on the effects of women's leadership groups moving together into liminal space for the sake of transition to deeper thought and experience.[2] I invited a small collective of women, then aged in their thirties and forties, to travel with me for two years in discussion and experimentation with their belief systems and behavior. The depth of inquiry and conversation waxed and waned over those two years, but we found ultimately that dialogue itself, within a clear circle of trust, a relational container, increased awareness of our assumptions and brought to the surface some deeply hidden beliefs about the roles of women in the home and in society. Heightened awareness about self and others led to changes in each participant: for some, as significant as career change and, for others, change in relational behavior and self-confidence. However, in the midst of the two years, the women found that they were angry, grieving, "lost" in some ways and caught in unhelpful stereotypes. The disruption to their lives as they realized sources of these feelings and perceptions did not provide for easy consciousness-raising and mobilization for change. Resistance and conflict became part of their life together as they lived in liminal space of self-discovery and relational work.

At the time of this writing, the women are no longer in touch with each other except at a superficial level due to geographical and career changes, as well as two untimely deaths. In individual conversations with several of the participants twenty years later, I have learned that our group work made a lasting impact on their decision making for intentional life-change. Consciousness-raising during the liminal space contained in our time together did indeed lead to mobilization for the majority of the women as they paid attention to the origins and impacts of their own belief systems in light of their greater contexts and desires.

Depolarization

Ideas about right and wrong, or conclusions about the way forward, or stereotypes of other persons all are called into question in this liminal space. What we have been taught and experiences that have shaped us come into the water with us, but they are also critiqued in liminal space.

I remember when I took a group of adults to South Africa from the United States for the purpose of cultural immersion. The participants had particular expectations. Many African

Americans in this group thought they were on pilgrimage to a place that was akin to their ancestral homeland. European Americans were prepared for blame as participants, passive or active, in apartheid; some were openly defensive, some guilt-ridden. As we traveled together in that liminal space, we found out how difficult our preconceived notions became for our relationships with each other. Those who expected welcome as cousins of South Africans were, in fact, considered by those they encountered to be US citizens and not related at all. Color of skin did not guarantee kinship. Those who were ready to deny any wrongdoing or to take the burden of blame learned that the alternative way forward was to fight for truth and reconciliation as a first step toward restorative justice in this so-called post-apartheid country.

All participants learned that in the early twenty-first century, South Africa was beginning to show signs of a continuation of economic apartheid along race lines despite a change in government that included fairer race representation. The group's expectations were turned on their heads because their preconceived ideas were disrupted. The result was group in-fighting, primarily along racial lines. As the leader, I could see that the group was mirroring the context in which we were living during those weeks, but I didn't know how to calm the waters so we could speak civilly with each other. Two group members seemed to be able to bridge the gap by keeping relations open. Others shut down. Still others took great issue with each other about attitudes and assumptions. We were in a whirlpool, drowning in the waters, while trying to find a familiar foothold by way of grasping at our prior relational interaction. Instead, we were entrenching and, for the most part, polarizing. No amount of pre-travel conversation about expectations prepared us for the experience of being together in a highly-charged situation. At that time, I was not prepared as a leader to keep us steady in the midst of the raging waters. It was an important lesson to learn about leadership in conflicted liminal space.

Since that trip, the most fractious immersion journey of the several I have led, I have learned a great deal about leadership in particularly disruptive liminal situations. I intentionally educated myself more deeply about what racism does to dominant and non-dominant peoples; I entered into conversations that were highly uncomfortable and received the rage of those who have experienced enough discrimination and side-lining to last several lifetimes. I have also sat with those who don't think racism exists anymore and even a very few who are not sure that the institution of slavery is unjustified in some countries. I have made choices about where I stand in deep solidarity and also choices about not polarizing or demonizing those who do not agree with me. Making such choices and sustaining them are hard; it's easier to demonize the "other," those who believe slavery isn't an ethically and morally wrong state of being, and only spend time with people who think like I do. I know that not all opinions are equal, and I know that, for me, the moral choice here is to support anti-racism movements. I also know that, if I never speak again to a proponent of racial segregation, then the world will continue its downward spiral of mutual destruction. That is not to say that I condone hate crimes or belief systems that hurt others or deny others freedom. Rather, I need to find out why these belief systems exist and how they emerged – what feeds them and how might we speak with each other without trying to "fix" each other, trying instead to soften the drawing of ever-deepening hard lines. How do I hold a space where differences can be aired honestly, yet civilly, with the intent that we respect stories and beliefs that have brought us to our current state of being? This held space is a figurative container that is created with the intention to build trust.

By contrast, were I to polarize the issues, I would continue to contribute to the problems we all have to face. Difference divided by stereotype and maintained by those invested in holding power stands strong as long as we stay in our safety zones. By entering the threshold of dangerous space, we are called into brave conversation, requiring courage and the willingness to change, starting with some compassion toward others with whom we seem to have little in common. Easier said than done. Yet, this work does need to occur in workplaces, schools, religious organizations, in families and in groups of people who gather for a cause. Without entering the threshold space, the polarization will worsen, violence will continue to increase, and we will be determined to create higher, wider, more electrically charged walls around our personal, local and national enclaves that destroy society and its people. Evidence of ceaseless wars and escalating terrorism is everywhere. This kind of violence occurs because of extreme polarization, based on belief systems and subsequent clashes of values that evolve into stereotypes about the intrinsic worth of people. Focusing on the worth of people replaces dealing with deep problems that are best faced collaboratively.

Take, for example, the tyrannical boss whom no one likes and everyone defames at the water cooler. Perhaps the boss deserves it and, undoubtedly, the employees may live in a hostile workplace. The boss becomes more and more isolated and out of touch with employees, and performance drops dramatically. The boss escalates threats to try to increase productivity. Employees keep their heads down and do what they are required to accomplish to get through the day. Nothing is working. Investment is low. The boss can't figure out what is wrong and fires people to try to get the right people in place. The cycle continues because the relational system is broken. What needs to happen is a culture change, and such a change will not happen if the boss and the employees cannot enter liminal space together, first, to de-polarize and, then, to take stock of what is happening in their interactions, with emerging intent to find a new way forward.

Disrupting this senseless cycle, which means stopping the blame-and-shame behavior in favor of looking toward the same purpose together, is crucial for relationships and for the business as a whole. As Brown says, "From corporations, nonprofits and public sector organizations to governments, activist groups, schools, and faith communities, we desperately need more leaders who are committed to courageous, wholehearted leadership and who are self-aware enough to lead from their hearts, rather than unevolved leaders who lead from hurt and fear."[3] A focus on purpose that addresses the needs of the stakeholders rather than the threat of internal relationships going awry shifts the system into a learning stance rather than a fear-based, command-and-control center.

Wheatley calls for circles of sanity in the midst of this great decline of civil relationship. She says, "We are not the first leaders to be stewarding a time of disintegration, fear, and loss. But none of us has been prepared for where we are."[4] Further, "Human societies always arrive at this place. It begins when we grow too large to remain as a community of intimate relationships. We shift from bonds of community to hierarchy; we organize into complex social relationships, with many different institutional structures and roles."[5] Circles, or islands of sanity, can occur only when we pull ourselves into a space where we encounter challenges to our own belief systems and stereotypes, albeit without sacrificing our moral choices. Again, Wheatley reminds us: "It is possible, in this time of profound disruption, for leadership to be a noble profession that contributes to the common good. . . . It is possible to use our influence and power to create *islands of* sanity in the midst of a raging destructive sea."[6]

In these spaces, if we listen deeply enough and with a posture of curiosity, we find that there is indeed a fundamental commonality, even if our journeys are different, a phenomenon that Carl Jung calls the collective unconscious, a liminal space that spans both geography and time. In the midst of the COVID-19 crisis, there was an unfolding awareness of our commonality across the globe, whether resulting in competition or crisis-care, but with certain understandings that no human being was entirely safe from infection. The collective unconscious turned to survival tactics deeply embedded in our human psyche—hoard as much as possible and also help as much as possible. We continue to learn in this century what it means to hold the collective in our awareness on a global scale.

Tuning in to the Collective Unconscious

Carl Jung (1875-1961), an analytical psychologist, created the pyschologically-based concept of the collective unconscious and the importance of symbols for human development. He moved beyond materialism – the notion that, if we can't identify physical manifestations of a phenomena, then it doesn't exist – and embraced the mystical and the intuitive in his work. Based on a dream where Jung explored several floors of a house, and then descended to its deepest depths where there was a cave filled with skulls from an ancient culture, he believed that he had stumbled upon an image of the psyche. The upper floor symbolized his conscious personality, the ground floor was the first level of unconsciousness and the floor underground was his collective unconscious, the common psychic heritage of all humanity:[7]

> What Jung was proposing was no less than a fundamental concept on which the whole science of psychology could be built. Potentially, it is of comparable importance to quantum theory in physics. Just as the physicist investigates particles and waves, and the biologist genes, so Jung held it to be the business of psychologists to investigate the collective unconscious and the functional unities of which it is composed – the *archetypes*, as he eventually called them.[8]

Archetypes are the larger-than-life, yet unseen, internal structures that manifest themselves in the common behavior and experience of all human beings throughout time. More recent understandings of archetypes claim that there are journeys necessary for each individual to mature into adulthood, based on what he or she needs to learn in terms of ancient wisdom:[9]

> Thus, on appropriate occasions, archetypes give rise to similar thoughts, images, mythologems, feelings, and ideas in people, irrespective of their class, creed, race, geographical location, or historical epoch. An individual's entire archetypal endowment makes up the collective unconscious, whose authority and power is vested in a central nucleus, responsible for integrating the whole personality, which Jung termed the Self.[10]

Examples of the archetype include heroes, mothers of the universe, the mentor, the innocent, the visionary, the scapegoat, the villain and the world redeemer. One can find mythologies

and modern stories with various archetypal characters in
them; films and adventure narratives, such as Star Wars[11] and
Harry Potter, fairy tales for children, folk stories from different
regions of the world and great tales and dramas from Dante,
the Beowulf poet and Shakespeare, all encompass patterns of
behavior and situations we can relate to at some deep level.
The heroes or heroines are the most popular figures of all –
Robin Hood, Braveheart, Hercules, Superman, and Wonder
Woman are powerful icons who rush in to save the day.

Joseph Campbell, an expert in comparative mythology
and greatly influenced by Jung, connected archetypes with
the collective unconscious through his life-long studies of
anthropology, psychology and mythology. He was convinced
that humanity had a psychic unity in its attempt to find a way
to the transcendent. For both Jung and Campbell, mythologies
carried metaphors that pointed beyond the world perceived by
the five senses. The hero or heroine's journey is what he calls
the "monomyth," the story from which all other archetypes are
derived.[12] There is a sequence involved in the hero's journey.
The hero or heroine is born of a special mother, with innate,
unique powers that manifest themselves over time. The journey
is the motif for self-discovery for the hero and heroine. This
journey in its many versions tells of initial suffering, followed
by an immersion in liminal space (my words), where he or she
encounters the transcendent through trials and learning. The
hero or heroine is transformed and returns home with great
power, enough to triumph and set society free. It does not take a
huge leap to see the connection between the rituals van Gennep
studied and Victor Turner further analyzed in terms of spiritual
emphases to see this kind of journey as part of an unconscious
collective understanding of human formation and maturation.

To recognize the collective unconscious requires a tuning in
to a deep human, and, indeed, creaturely, knowledge that has
been enriched throughout the eons. The collective unconscious
surpasses current trends and knowledge in its wisdom.
Liminal space calls for a deepened listening to this collective
wisdom and experience throughout time. Spiritual leaders
increasingly call for this kind of listening, currently described
as "mindfulness," or paying attention to what is right in front

of us and ascribing meaning to it. However, Jung would go deeper than mindfulness. Tuning in to collective unconscious is not merely a personal practice or individual attending to the present. It is a joining in the flow of human consciousness that is already born in us, like DNA, with the experience of eons behind it. It is swimming in water that has been present since the dawn of humanity. Some of this collective unconscious emerges as a deep instinct, most evident today in the animal realm. Some of it is felt intuition or "gut knowing" about the unspoken phenomena behind what appear to be uncommon, yet explicable occurrences; in other words, a first-time experience can seem oddly familiar.

Even leadership analysts are tapping into what found of the Global Leadership Iniitiative, Joseph Jaworski, and others are calling the "Source." He quotes Robert Jahn and Brenda Dunne, two scientists he interviewed for his own work, *Source: The Inner Path of Knowledge Creation*:

> There exists a much deeper and more extensive source of reality, which is largely insulated from direct human experience, representation, or even comprehension. It is a domain that has long been posited and contemplated by metaphysicians and theologians, Jungian and Jamesian psychologists, philosophers of science, and a few contemporary progressive theoretical physicists, all struggling to grasp and to represent its essence and its function. A variety of provincial labels have been applied, such as "Tao," "Qi," "prana," "void," "Akashic record," "Unus Mundi," "unknowable substratum," "terra incognita," "archetypal field," "hidden order," "aboriginal sensible muchness," "implicate order," "zero point vacuum," "ontic (or ontological level)," "undivided timeless primordial reality," among many others, none of which fully captures the sublimely elusive nature of this domain. In earlier papers we called it the "subliminal seed regime," but for our present purposes we shall henceforth refer to it as the "Source."[13]

Liminal space, threshold space, is primarily about tuning in to that which we might not otherwise notice in our hectic lives, lives inundated with messages about popularity, consumption, opinion polls, polarization and competition. The voices of others who have different experiences, yet paradoxically ones that we all share at some level, create the common ground upon which we stand, or common river in which we swim, which includes a collective sense of trying to make meaning of life. Ancient "knowing" (a Source) reverberates in this space, as van Gennep's tribes can demonstrate to us. The boy who is sent into the wilderness without instruction has to tap into ways of survival that are not outlined for him by his elders. He has to use what he knows through mimicking what he has seen, but he also has to take the initiative and follow intuition to make his own decisions and develop his own path to become the adult.

Those who pay attention to ancestral rituals and stories are likely to bring this knowledge with them. Those who are taught individualism and subsequent competition pointed toward personal success are unlikely to understand what is available to all of us.

Storytelling is the most common way for human beings to tap into our commonality. There are stories that reach deeply into us and that seem to have a deeply rooted wisdom beyond time constraints. The hero/heroine journey stories tap into Jung's archetypes about life-trajectories for men and women, the former stepping out on a quest to find self (into liminal space) and the latter, first questing for deep roots where she is free of patriarchal limitations (also liminal space) to set out on such a journey.

Mythologies often carry these archetypal "knowings" of the collective unconscious, whether stories about salvific figures or the stereotypically weak figure winning against the strong. Ultimately, tapping into the collective unconscious is liminal and moves us toward our inner essence or soul. This immersion serves to move us beyond creating competitive polarities and carries us deeper into waters of shared connection. Then we move deeper still as we continue to explore threshold waters.

Inner Essence or Soul Work

Inner essence or soul comprises one part of our beings. Inner work is messy because it is not easily defined like body and mind can be. Inner essence is the place where connecting with the collective unconscious occurs, where we find our groundedness, sometimes named our "center," or a spiritual higher power relevant to one's faith-system. Inner essence has an intuitive and ephemeral quality and cannot be attributed to thoughts and physicality, though it may signal with particular awarenesses to our brains and bodies at times. Instinct comes to play in the inner essence; we can learn well from animals here. Flight, fight or freeze in danger, search for sustainable food sources and cycles of life and death all come from this inner essence that has its home in the collective unconscious of each species.

Inner essence or soul is the deepest part of our being. It is also the easiest to ignore amidst all the noise in our heads and hearts, as well as the onslaught of messaging and conflict we face every day. The rise of countless people encouraging mindfulness and meditation through online courses and local gatherings speaks to the sense of loss we are experiencing in dominant, Western cultures. We have lost our groundedness. Responses to this loss are exhibited by the numbers of people joining gangs, employing addictive substances, and starting crusades against whole sectors of humanity (e.g., white supremacists, anti-gay movements, silencers of women's justice movements). Living in despair or meaninglessness and striving for personal power are twins; neither of them looks deeply into the groundedness of our collective being.

Of course, there are different approaches to soul work, depending on our preferences with regard to how we gain energy, absorb information, prioritize our relationships and work and organize ourselves. Some people prefer to experience life simply, others want to immerse themselves in imagination and the arts; some want to think about philosophies and analyze them and others focus on personal meaning and supportive relationships.[14] Pragmatism, imagination, reason and emotions all contribute to the soul work of which we are capable, often fueled by nature, beauty, music and the other arts. Unfortunately, many people have become hardened against experiences, considering them "soft" and for a certain "type" of person. Here, the ugly side of individualism rears its head again as people think they can control their lives without attention to grounded being.

This attentiveness to inner essence or soul in the midst of in-between space and time helps us delve into the deepest of life's concerns: living with reality in both its positive and negative elements, determining our purpose for existing during our brief lifetime, establishing values that guide our actions and interactions, relating to experiences with other human beings and the natural world, knowing we are not alone and having human agency.[15] Ultimately, our human interconnectedness leads to a desire to learn more about the world in which we live, fostered by a curiosity about what we might be missing, as well as what might surprise us as we journey. People from different social locations, different parts of the world, different stages of life and even surprising events all can be incorporated into our soul journeys when we remain open in liminal space.

We are creatures who are meant to be connected, to belong to each other and the planet. As Irish poet-scholar John O'Donohue says, "The hunger to belong is at the heart of our nature. Cut off from others, we atrophy and turn in on ourselves. The sense of belonging is the natural balance of our lives."[16] To be connected with each other and with the earth, its elements and its creatures, we have to find the deepest part of ourselves that knows who we are before we can encounter those who are not like us. This inner "knowing" is the groundedness that keeps us steady in the midst of uncertainty, disruption and adventuresome exploration. We no longer are defined by our roles, jobs or other people's opinions even when we participate in all these areas. Liminal work requires that we find our center, our grounding, so that we may accompany others in their own search as we are accompanied, which is the very nature of belonging together. In other words, we can't swim completely alone forever without losing our sanity.

The most grounded person I know is a small business owner who has also worked in the social agency sector. Blandy has raised two sons, has very clear boundaries with clients and family and has well-thought-out belief systems. She meditates, advocates for those who cannot advocate for themselves, is an expert in the healing arts and has a no-nonsense attitude complete with raucous sense of humor. Blandy also is a consummate storyteller and has learned to care about a deeply wounded world without succumbing to its pain. In other words, she is very clear about her grounding and claims a source of energy outside herself as her focus for her center. People either gravitate toward her wisdom or avoid her because she does not acquiesce to others' opinions unless given good reason. She does not suffer fools gladly. I consider her a friend and mentor because she is wise. She has clear understanding of how one enters liminal space as needed or as called into it, naming this space transformative, while existing as a solidly grounded person. Without being a student of Carl Jung, she is deeply rooted in the collective unconscious in her wisdom, exhibiting connection to ancient sources of wisdom in her healing practice.[17]

Transformation

The word "transformation" has seen a reinvigoration recently. The traditional definition gives the word some general parameters: "change in form, appearance, nature, or character."[18] For some leaders, transforming means changing radically or significantly. Transformation is a hoped-for outcome in many group processes, retreats or rituals. How people define transformation varies depending on the starting point and arrival into a new space. The process of transformation, no matter how it is defined and whether it does indeed happen, occurs in liminal space. The fruits of transformation are seen once one leaves liminal space and assimilates to and reflects on a new reality.

Transforming, much like the word "liminal," implies movement across or transition ("trans" means across, beyond, through) or changing thoroughly. Indeed, this definition relates closely to what one could encounter in liminal space, traversing from one state of being to another through awareness-raising, learning and mobilization. Like water that flows, freezes, melts, vaporizes, flows and freezes again, there is a cycle to this transforming work in liminal space.

Many speakers and authors considering leadership issues spend time addressing skill sets and outcomes, using linear action/consequence models. Leaders who are primarily learners tend to focus on changing organizations via transforming employee relationships with each other and with the work itself throughout the hierarchy, moving beyond skill sets to a more significant change in ways of thinking altogether. Change theory in the twenty-first century is beginning to focus on deeper levels of awareness and learning by urging leaders to make themselves present to the world as one actor within a larger whole. There is almost an "inner essence" and "collective unconscious" or "Source" quality to this approach in the business world. Thinkers called futurists are tapping into this sense of learning in exciting ways, which Peter Senge and colleagues call the "emerging future":

> We've come to believe that the core capacity needed to access the field of the future is presence. We first thought of presence as being fully conscious and aware in the present moment. Then we began to appreciate presence as deep listening, of being open beyond one's preconceptions and historical ways of making sense. We came to see the importance of letting go of old identities and the need to control and, as Salk said, making choices to serve the evolution of life. Ultimately, we came to see all these aspects of presence as leading to a state of "letting come," of consciously participating in a larger field for change.[19]

At a personal level, transformation occurs when we pay attention to the soul work mentioned above. Significant change moves us into a new reality as we break out of the prisons we have constructed for ourselves by others' expectations, ideas that keep us "in a box," internalized fear and guilt or desire for power over others. While dwelling in liminal space, we are capable of naming the chains that hold us by our own willingness to allow our minds to be captive, whether our bodies are free or not. Sometimes what begins as freedom can over time become captivity. The chains slowly close in. At the point of awareness, when we realise that we are at a point where the chains are too tight, we reach a place of choice. We continue, bound, or we change. When we choose change, we begin to loosen the chains and wake up to the freedom of adventure and the gifts before us.[20] This awakening can be called the first step of transformation. If this work is intentionally done together, in a group of people who are willing to do it, whether in the business world or the religious world or any place of work or study, then transformative conversations are subsequently followed by transformative events.

A friend of mine, Sandy, formerly vice president of strategic planning in a Fortune 500 company, enjoyed the excitement (and long hours) of her work over eighteen years that ultimately led to her becoming one of the senior executives in the company. Over the years, she began to feel disgruntled about decisions being made by the company, as well as an inner stirring to follow a call to Christian ministry. Meanwhile, she fostered deeper awareness by immersing herself in work trips that made a difference to those living in poverty, volunteering in an organization that serves victims of violent crime, speaking with those whom she trusted and taking time to discern. When the CEO of the company decided to move its headquarters out of state for reasons that did not make much sense to Sandy, she decided to leave and follow the call to ministry by enrolling in a theological seminary. A new freedom and sense of adventure arose and she encountered a new working community, making a spiritual difference in the world. She continues to use her business acumen with social service and religious groups and has found her way as a community leader, practicing compassion and assistance freely wherever the need arises. Such is the work that occurs in liminal space and the transformation that can occur when one walks into the threshold waters.[21]

Positives and Negatives

Of course, entering liminal space has its positive and negative aspects. Connecting with an undefined space that is different from what one knows, but not quite where one hopes to be, is risky. Each component of liminality requires personal vulnerability, a willingness to take chances and fail, perhaps a knowledge that one will encounter anger and rejection for a time. Without an inner anchor or center, this space seems wildly unfocused and disorganized. People often run away as fast as they can or entrench in their normal, familiar dwelling space rather than take on something that might create change. There is no map and, for some, there is no tolerance for uncharted territory without trying to lay out steps, behavior, goals and outcome rubrics. There is warrant for these actions in controlled strategic planning, but they are not the path to transformation *per se*.

Liminal space can *unintentionally* happen to anyone. Tragedy strikes. Bad things happen. We are required to recalibrate our lives and our thinking. *Intentional* dwelling in liminal space is called for when transition presents itself or is needed, and one enters a reflective and interactive time-space that requires discernment and listening. It is difficult to quieten the internal and external demands to enter this space, especially given the demands of everyday life. Yet, to foster connections with others in a transforming way, counter to the polarizing tendencies found everywhere, one taps first into the collective unconscious with inner essence or soul work. All of these components of liminal space disrupt us, calling us to nourish our roots and to be the best human beings we can be – adventuresome, flourishing, free and centered, despite living in an insane and over-controlling world. Such intention is hard work, often filled with grief as well as joy.

We return to our water metaphor. Water is dangerous. In extreme conditions, it perpetuates flood and, in hill-country, mudslide. It ruins crops and destroys homes. It soaks and disintegrates solids. It drowns creatures. It can shape itself into a tsunami, destroying vast areas of land and all who dwell there. Liminal space can also be so suddenly disruptive that it endangers us. That is why we move into it with our reference point of who we are, grounding us to encounter gentle waves or survive an onslaught of water capable of threatening our way of living. To open to what lies ahead, whatever it may be, frees us to encounter gifts we cannot yet see in the emerging future. We have crossed into the threshold and encountered its initial possibilities and dangers. Next, we familiarize ourselves with liminal space's boundaries.

"Splitting open"
New Zealand, 2015

Chapter Three

Learning the Intentional Containing Space

The banks of a river provide a constant structure that allows water freedom to flow and bounce and sparkle in a chaotic dance of balance and beauty.
– Eila Carrico[1]

One important facet of the middle or transitional space is its boundaries. When we are in unfamiliar territory, we try to find its extent, its walls or the containment of its space so that we are not free-floating without the potential for an anchor. We want to know our parameters. We need something solid to hold onto in the midst of flow, especially if the waters are moving quickly and unpredictably. Sometimes we turn to friends or family to hold us steady; other times we repeat phrases we learned long ago to make some kind of explanation for tragedy. When disruption occurs, we try and find something that "contains" or eases our fear and anxiety.

With our water metaphor, we focus on the flow itself, not passively going along to get along, but to learn from the flow and to tap into what is already all around us creating enough safety that we can "live into" the movement, whether fast, turbulent, slow or smooth. Think about where water goes. The wellspring flows into the stream which flows into the river which flows to the lake or the great sea. In this flow, we find ourselves moving along particular paths that are contained by land: the hole through which the water rises from deep within the earth, the banks of the stream, the river- or lake-bed, the delta and the ocean floor. The rock and soil that contain the water's flow are aligned with it, but also are affected by it; rock and soil are agile because they move as they are eroded by the pressure of the water. However, the changing container does not mean it disappears. Water is contained in some fashion or the entire globe would be inundated with it, and only water creatures and plants could survive.

The nature of a container is that of a solid that holds something else that is either a smaller solid, liquid or gas. The container gives shape to the substance it surrounds or covers a substance to protect it and keep it from deteriorating as quickly as it otherwise might. It aligns with what it contains, holding it in a particular shape and place.

Liminal space, the in-between "this" or "that," and a combination of "this" and "that," is surrounded in temporal terms. In other words, there is a starting point and an end point that define the middle space. Yet, there is more to containing this space than its beginning and ending. To navigate the unknown well, we bring our inner knowledge and habits with us at the starting place where we cross into threshold. In intentional liminality, we also may need a skilled facilitator to "hold space" when there is work to be done. Otto Scharmer, mentioned in Chapter One, describes this container in *Theory U* as a circle of relationship that must be "charged" with two elements: unconditional care that is listening without judgment with an open spirit and the courage to let go and surrender.[2] If the facilitator can charge the container in this way and invite others to do so, then the collective presence is a different quality than a conversation group or a meeting; the group has entered liminal space where people's former selves are included and their future selves are emerging. Many awareness-raising or creativity circles know this principle to be true.

Gestalt theory uses this understanding of "container" in its practice of encountering the whole person in dialogue. When the coach or therapist initiates a relational field between her or him and the client(s) by raising awareness of surroundings, staying in the present moment and listening actively, this is considered a "container."[3] Amy Edmondson, Professor of Leadership and Management at Harvard Business School, adds that psychological safety is important in a container and necessary for any learning to occur:

> In psychologically safe environments, people believe that, if they make a mistake, others will not penalize or think less of them for it. They also believe that others will not resent or humiliate them when they ask for help or information. . . . Psychological safety does not imply a cozy situation in which people are necessarily close friends. Nor does it suggest an absence of pressure or problems.[4]

Similarly, Mary Pierce Brosmer, founder of *Women Writing for (a) Change* and consultant for transformational work to business organizations and schools, has spent decades developing leadership through the art of writing. She defines the nature of the container as Scharmer does (and, indeed, refers to Scharmer, Wheatley, and others as influencers for her thinking).[5] She describes the work of the container as collecting a community in a particular place, with a ritual of gathering, being together and leave-taking. It is in the ritual that a circle is opened and then closed, with the time and space between opening and closing where the creative work, often transformative, takes place. A participative facilitator "holds the space," to allow others to express themselves as deeply as they are willing and able, relating rather than creating or identifying roles.[6] Brosmer says:

> By *container*, I mean the organizational universe, encompassing all aspects of how a group lives: time, physical space, money, relational agreements, food, and ritual. The word container has many analogues:

ecosystem, home, womb. Anything that maintains the
delicate balance between open space and boundaries
and allows life to emerge is the container.[7]

I joined one of the women's writing groups developed by
Brosmer during a particularly difficult season at one point in
my life, walking into the first meeting wounded and unsure
of my own next steps to free myself of a micromanaging
environment that affected my leadership in ways that countered
my creativity, growth and maturation. I also was grieving
how the environment was hurting the whole organization at
the time. I knew that my story was not unique; many have
experienced the pain of anxious organizations who do not
manage their collective anxiety well. I needed an outlet that
was safe and at the same time challenging so that I could find
my way out of a very unhealthy situation. A friend of mine
from another, similar organization invited me to attend her
group. I trusted her judgment and her facilitation from past
experience and so decided to spend the time and energy to
move into this writing-for-healing space.

My friend and another facilitator, both named Lisa, held
the container for the women gathered every Monday night
for twelve weeks. My friend did so by greeting us, lighting a
candle to pass around the circle as we named ourselves into
the space, reading a poem, having us write about something
in the poem that caught our attention, fostering small group
discussion which turned into deep sharing, more free-writing
time, reading our work to each other, then closing the circle by
naming what was important or what we noticed, followed by
passing the candle again, but in the opposite direction. What
seemed like a simple ritual became a powerful container,
allowing participants to delve more deeply each week into
the joys and pains of life, but also to discover both inner
and collective power that was indeed, transformative. Belief
systems shifted, minds changed, people who might have
been polarized about political or social issues found ways to
speak with each other with humor and care. I myself began to
develop a dream for my own work in the future, far away from
the workplace that was so toxic to me.

Without this contained space in which I found freedom to give myself permission to get a little wild with my dreaming, I am not sure that I would have found a new way forward, complete with educational re-tooling, coaching training and certification and creating new business networks. This circle was my liminal space and I worked hard, laughed, cried and felt anger and joy in it, because it was supportive, defined, and facilitated well, containing the creative flow just enough to allow freedom to reframe my perspective.[8]

The point here is not to emulate a writing circle for women or men, but to understand the nature of a container when an individual or group is on a journey in liminal space. A skilled facilitator creates a sense of intentionality in the midst of risk, through a trajectory of time spent with a great deal of freedom built in. There is welcome and closure at each gathering, drawing people in and then sending them back into the world for a time but, with new insight or new questions, complete with a subsequent action plan for change. The space is dialogical, with parameters set for adopting a learning posture, while at the same time honoring one's own self. The space also needs to be honored for a time so that growth and, ultimately, transformation has potential to evolve – the future emerges this way, paradoxically contained and free.

Practical Matters
FACILITATING A LEARNING TEAM IN LIMINAL SPACE – THE LEADER

There are several roles in containers. First, the facilitator-leader creates the atmosphere that both provides safety and invites risk of vulnerability and letting go. She or he participates briefly by not only creating the foundation for the conversation or silence by example, but also doing so without losing the sense of guiding the process for the sake of all others present. The intention is to create in-between space where generative conversation can occur.

When tensions rise, the facilitator acknowledges them and makes sure that voices are honored respectfully; listening is more important than speaking in these spaces, though speaking one's own truth also matters greatly. Friction is likely to arise in vulnerable spaces when a deep belief system is revealed, accompanied by the deep emotions that have shaped the belief in the first place. Thus, when vulnerability is tested, people are taking a chance that they will not be attacked or manipulated by persons with differing belief systems. Such attacks occur frequently in our society; witness reports in the broadcast media and newspaper press of attacks on and by public figures, hate groups, and in work conflicts, family conflicts and, yes, Facebook threads. The need to be correct and the ingrained need to "win" in competitive cultures can make vulnerability a liability rather than a gift. Zero-sum thinking, where one cannot win unless someone else loses, makes sense in the realm of sports but does not have to be the model businesses follow, especially with internal personnel. Changing the world for the better by finding unique niches and complementary industries serves a higher purpose promoting powerful, positive change.

To foster trust, a facilitator invites bravery in a space that has some very clear guidelines about how people will communicate and honor each other. The group itself can create an agreement about how it operates as long as this honoring of others' voices is included. Otherwise, the dynamic will never transcend either uniformity or disgruntlement and some people will remain closed and fearful while others dominate the conversation. Over time, as conversation and shared presence deepens, the agreement may become outdated and need to be revised. If trust is shared among participants and if the facilitator is trusted, then people begin to learn new things while letting go of old things, difficult as that may be, such as foundations for belief systems or self-images that may not serve them or anyone else well on individual and organizational levels alike.

Belief systems are often very strong because they are foundations for our thoughts and behavior. At some level, they served us well. However, as we grow, we receive new information and experience new events. Beliefs need to grow with the expansion of knowledge and experience. However, change at this level can shake one's whole world. A container holds the space and the flow enough that deep change can be possible without overwhelming a person or a whole system.

For example, I have encountered many persons of faith who insist that the (positive) behavior of the Church should never change because Jesus created the Church in a certain way. The only change since Jesus' time is modern plumbing, technology, automobiles and church architecture. When they begin to understand that Jesus did not create the Church and was not a Christian, their belief systems crumble. They have a choice at this point. They can fight the information that has been revealed and insist that their teaching from childhood stands, or they can adopt a sense of curiosity, perhaps in the midst of grief at letting go of long-held assumptions, and find out more. A skilled facilitator will gently foster their curiosity without judging the assumptions held for a lifetime. If people trust the facilitator, they are more likely to learn and move to a new system of beliefs.

People are greatly helped if there is ritual in business meetings or family gatherings, especially in times of disruption or discord. In times of crisis, ritual is even more important, whether performed as a steadying habit, or invented as a new focus for grounding in the midst of fear. In fact, ritual whether secular or religious, helps people trust that the space they enter is predictable enough that it will indeed "hold" them should the unpredictable insight, revelation, or conflict occur. Rituals might include a certain way of greeting as each enters the space, or a certain question or reading that begins the time together. Rituals include a reminder of purpose, honoring time and relationship, and conclude with a prompt, appropriate ending that consistently has a sending forth element to it. Closing container space and time with a promise to meet again as scheduled, without exception, provides a foundation from which people can take risks. Group centering in this way allows the individual to center in her or his own being, which makes risk possible.

PARTICIPATING IN A GROUP IN LIMINAL SPACE

Whether participating as an employee, or through common interest, with friends or to converse with people from other cultures, those who cross into the work of transformation by wanting to move beyond their current home of belief need to encounter some of the limits and also freedoms of the container. Boundaries are set for protection; freedom is open for searching and creative curiosity based on all that each participant brings to the table. Thus, liminal space is begun and liminal thinking can occur.

Dave Gray asserts, "There are opportunities around you all the time, every day, and, in many cases, you are unable to see them, because limiting belief blinds you to real possibilities. Liminal thinking is a way to identify limiting beliefs and open yourself to hitherto unseen possibilities that can open new doors."[9] Before such shifts can occur, one has to be involved in the right container. One also has to be willing to bring the whole self to the group occupying this space after a natural testing period to ascertain if trust is possible.

To begin the journey into in-between space, a number of preconditions need to exist. If someone is interested in maintaining her or his lens on the world without exception, whatever the motive for doing so (and there are many), and if this desire is reinforced by a person's surroundings and relationships, then there is little incentive to change personally, professionally, or relationally. In this case, liminal work is not right for the moment unless a person is forced into change by external, unintentional disruption. Therefore, the first precondition to participation in threshold work is to recognize one's own inability to know what one doesn't know or experience what one has not (yet) encountered. After realizing one's incapacity to know and experience all perspectives, naming naming a problematic stance that has heretofore been assumed to be universally true coupled with a desire to expand one's thinking, then the most crucial step for liminal work has taken place. Business leaders and teams, nonprofit organizations, religious congregations and various social-political movements all must meet this precondition before voluntarily entering liminal space with positive intent.

Another precondition is the willingness to hear and recount stories. In the business world, in particular, stories occur over lunch or during breaks but rarely in the meeting room, unless they are tools in presenting a particular proposal or evaluative point. Stories in other sectors play a more vital role in the day-to-day work of employees, volunteers or networks. Telling stories as anecdotes on the frontlines in the midst of crisis eases the sense of being alone and helps mitigate potential burnout. Liminal space requires storytelling to uncover the truth about each other while building relationships or responding to an emergency, whether engaging a working relationship that has potential for more depth and creativity, or a more informal relationship that is deepening and broadening networks. With storytelling come emotive responses, which may vary among participants. Allowing for different responses is essential, acknowledging that one's own worldview or belief system should not, and cannot, dominate the conversation and yet should not be subordinate to it either.

This leads us to the final precondition. Liminal space is filled with a diversity of belief systems, some of which may be based on social location (all those qualities that we have inherited or learned, physical and mental, including race, gender, sexuality, culture, religion, education level and economic class), some of which may be based on life-mindset (such as values that are couched in fear, love, adventure, anger, contentment and so on). To participate fully and to walk toward transformation, one has to expect to encounter difference. The awkwardness that almost always automatically arises from this encounter with diversity creates a desire within the group to diffuse it, which either leads to creative conversation and innovation or to conflict and shutdown. Finding common ground while honoring difference is an act unto itself that begins a transformative process for people; however, one must be capable of living a learning posture, open to questioning and curiosity about self and others without reverting into defensiveness or denial.

In other words, curiosity and a spirit of exploration may be nascent at the cusp of liminal space but, with good facilitation and commitment from participants, these learning postures expand as people move more deeply into the depths of their being by telling the stories they carry within them. Some of these stories may never have been told before, which often leads to a breakthrough for the teller and perhaps the listener. They also lead to innovations in belief systems and perspectives, which in turn can change the direction of businesses, their products and the audiences they target, the foci and work approach of nonprofit organizations and the nature of spiritual presences in community.

At the same time, learning postures do not negate belief systems that may be important to sustain. One does not enter liminal space to lose identity but to change one's understanding of identity. Our foundational center remains grounded in a very broad sense. For example, if one approaches this space with an ethic of love that has not seen the light of day for some time due to work pressures and exhaustion, then the space calls forth this deep, inner conviction rather than trying to change it. When the depth of our best self comes forth, we are capable of changing beliefs, worldview and behavior without losing ourselves to conformity or uniformity. Herein lies the personal container, or an ultimate unshakeability, which some might call safety, as differentiated from the group container. Acknowledging one's deepest awareness, value and passion on a personal level breaks through our normal self-protection in liminal space and, in turn, contributes meaningfully to the liminal work of the team or group:

> Getting clear on our value and our team members' values will revolutionize our company and create lanes where none might have existed before – instead of a ten-person race, we start to develop a coordinated relay in which team members baton-toss to each other's strengths instead of vying to run the whole stretch alone. Once everyone understands their value, we stop hustling for worthiness and lean into our gifts.[10]

These commitments to awareness, value, and passion influence each other into a higher, more complex way of knowing and experiencing, thereby moving individuals and teams into the threshold of transformational work.

Unintentional Liminal Space

During extreme duress, such as living through natural disasters, global pandemics, market crashes, terrorist attacks, lethal or maiming hate crimes, unexpected deaths or, in many countries, genocide, civil war, refugee movements, immigration "trains" and unaccounted for "disappearances" of the citizenry, people are thrown into liminal space. Life will never be what it was hours or days ago and the future is uncertain and perhaps unimaginable.

It is in these times that we see the worst and best of humanity. Some take full advantage of others' loss, grief and pain, making money or media soundbites on the back of victims or exploiting difficult situations for personal, often financial, gain. The opposite is also true. Others rally to support, advocate and provide alternatives for victims, working hard to move with them from victimhood to survival. Victims themselves often rally together so that they know they are not alone. The sense of belonging is crucial when people experience shock and are thrown into deep loss and uncertainty. Trauma like this can affect one person, a group, whole populations and countries. COVID-19, the global pandemic landing at the beginning of a new decade (2020), resulted in varied responses. Some world leaders were quick to provide testing and protect the population as much as they could, and others brushed off the problem until it became so dire that escalating death tolls devastated nation-states. People were quarantined, "sheltering in place," all over the world. Panic ruled the airwaves and social media. At the same time, something else emerged: new ways of creating community, advancing technologies and their uses, and understandings of how to remain social in the midst of physical distancing. The impacts of the pandemic still remain to be seen over the next decades, but it is clear that business-as-usual is long gone and that the entire globe is in disrupted, liminal space. The great curiosity will be what the new equilibrium looks like even as we move through chaos, fear, and grief.

Another example of extreme disruption, one of many in history, is the Lisbon earthquake of 1755, which changed the life of the Portuguese population and also had lasting impact on European understanding of religion and social life. Lisbon was one of the five largest cities in Europe at that time and an important coastal trading center for Europe. The whole population of Lisbon, with estimated instant losses of 70,000 people, was catapulted into instant liminality.[11] The earthquake struck while much of the population was in church on All Saints' Day, which exacerbated the religious and psychological trauma:

Stone churches collapsed onto their congregations.
The royal palace and many stone mansions crumbled.
The ocean pulled back to expose the rubble on the floor
of the harbor, and the tsunami scoured the waterfront
portions of the city. Fires began that burned for several
days. Tens of thousands died. It was a huge earthquake,
centered on the Atlantic floor, estimated at nine on the
Richter scale, devastating as far away as Morocco, felt
as far away as northern Europe, with tsunami waves
that reached Ireland and North Africa.[12]

One of Portugal's chief ministers, serving under King José I,
used this liminal space-time to update building codes and evict
the Jesuits with whom he had political difficulty. Theological
debates broke out all over Europe about natural disasters and
the all-powerful God. Political and religious or ideological
change occurred because of this great upheaval. Social scientist
and anthropologist Bjørn Thomassen, describes the earthquake
as having ramifications at every level of human life, shaking
the optimism of Europe's philosophers and religious leaders:
". . . as a single rupture, it exerted a huge impact on Europe's
intellectual life. It helped to shape the entire Enlightenment. It
was a formative impact on a series of thinkers, including Kant."[13]

Leaders who know how to navigate this kind of liminal
space are crucial in times of disruption and disaster; good
leaders command and control in wise ways, simply to work
for the victims' survival in pandemics, natural disasters, or
other times when evacuation or an immediate plan for physical
safety is needed. Liminal space is forced on victims. Rescue
workers respond by navigating the physical space. There are
also leaders who do the emotional and spiritual work with
those experiencing extreme disruption; they come as the second
wave of response. In these situations, creating a container of
(relative) safety is essential to ease people through shock, grief,
despair and the gamut of emotions accompanying shattering
change. Then there are leaders who begin to interpret the event
and respond to it, either for good or for ill. These leaders shape
the future of the belief system held by much of the population
affected, as well as those who hear about the events on the news.

I am reminded of the visit I made to El Salvador in 2008 with a small group of students from all walks of life, right before a political change in government occurred in 2009, when the Farabundo Martí National Liberation Front (FMLN) came to power. It did not take long to see that the entire country was in a state of post-traumatic stress as a result of ongoing Nationalist Republican Alliance (ARENA) violence and guerrilla response. We spent some time with a Roman Catholic sister working in some of the villages there. She knew every villager's personal story and she gave us the hard facts regarding the level of suffering the people had endured, watching from their hiding places as their village was destroyed and family members were shot. Sister Peggy introduced us to the few survivors in that particular region. Each time we made the acquaintance of these (mostly) young teenagers, she asked them to tell us their story. At first, I responded internally with my Midwestern-US sensibility that dictated my not intruding into others' lives. I also knew that I wasn't sure I could hear the horror and not break down. I realized after hearing two stories, with many more yet to come, that Sister Peggy had asked her friends to tell their experiences in as much detail as they could remember for a reason. She also asked us not to interrupt or ask questions.

In Sister Peggy's view, though controversial among trauma response experts, storytelling was the first step the traumatized speakers could take toward any semblance of healing after their violent separation from land and loved ones, life as they knew it.[14] Our listening honored the importance of each person's experience and, at the same time, forced us to listen and learn. Their violently unintentional liminal space created our own, at least for those who did not shut down. Our political stances aside, many of us suddenly found ourselves unable to breathe, weeping openly, unable to look each other in the eye, filled with the deepest empathy and horror we have ever felt. A few group members did put up emotional barriers to the tales of atrocity, no longer participating in the trip, staying behind at our hostels to read novels and take naps unless we were traveling. Group dissent arose at the two different responses to the extreme stories, which I addressed as something the group needed to discuss in my presence. Several students chose not to do so. It was easy for me to see the beginnings of group polarization and I knew that I needed to create a container where we could speak to each other honestly rather than shutting down.

Eventually, the entire group did come together to discuss how we all came to the situation with different capacities for listening and response based on our own worldviews and life-experiences in those weeks. However, only those who were committed to reflecting on what they had heard with open hearts were able to change their beliefs and worldviews. The others were not ready or, perhaps, not willing. The group still needed to honor these differences amidst the frustration, difficult as it was for them and me. To this day, one member of the group, Jay, a former corporate manager and now religious leader, regularly returns to El Salvador because his capacity for empathy and desire for solidarity blossomed in response to the pain he heard and saw. Before the trip, Jay was resentful that an academic degree requirement had forced him to travel at an inconvenient time. After the trip, he named his connection with the Salvadoran peoples through their stories and history as life-changing for him. Indeed, on one occasion he raised his own resources to travel there on the eve of a Salvadoran government election (2009) to aid the United Nations as an electoral observer.[15]

Such is the transformational nature of liminal space, which in this case was a cultural immersion trip that witnessed the forced liminality of those who had lost everything. It is a complex space, often emotionally charged and deeply painful until one is capable of enough reflection to make some meaning of, in this case, suffering and violent loss. Listening with learning posture, openness to internal and external change and a welcoming of difference create the right conditions for transformation, even in extreme circumstances.

Positives and Negatives

Entering liminal space, the middle or in-between transition from one state to another creates tremendous potential for transformation in one's thinking and experience, therefore shifting one's belief system. At the same time, this space evokes the best self from deeply held convictions that may manifest themselves in new, more open and, perhaps, healthier ways. In other words, a person encountering the in-between is quite capable of moving, like a boat in the flow of water, without being easily swayed by the prevailing wind. As the container for the space is held well, the work of entry and the development of learning postures and storytelling frameworks, with acceptance of diverse perspectives and social locations, can begin to take shape.

The caution here is that water erodes earth and rock, or earth and rock give way and the container suddenly changes. Sometimes the flow pushes hard against the container and people are not ready for the disruption that flow often brings, or they may not have the capacity for movement. They can't quite suspend their own belief systems or reframe traumatic experiences or they are indeed easily swayed by every opinion, every prevailing wind. As a result, in the first case, disruption shuts them down and the container is not enough; they must create their own, isolated sense of safety. Or, if they have no grounding at all, the container doesn't matter; they are simply along for the ride and not interested in gaining depth. Facilitators and other participants face these dynamics in liminal space and will need to address them directly. Those who cannot move or move at every whim are less likely to be creative contributors to the space, its focus, and its process. Instead, they will seek to preserve themselves, perhaps at the expense of others' lives and well-being.

Containers matter. They allow for the collective unconscious to arise, for the best in people to emerge and for the future to unfold in adventuresome ways when held well. They can sustain the forces of conflict, the sudden changes of direction, and be as flexible as they need to. Leaders who hold containers for liminal work are themselves grounded learners, sitting in the posture of curiosity as participants move into the next iteration of their best selves.

Part II

FACETS OF LIMINAL SPACE

In the path of water's flow, we encounter many adventures: new sights, sounds, curves and bends, pathway configurations, unexpected rapids and waterfalls, dams that slow us and waterways that veer off in their own directions. We may encounter temperature change as well. Ice and snow or steam are facets of water flow depending on earth, heat levels and pressure. These components of water as a substance begin to connect on the journey in liminal space. Encounter in the midst of liminal space is a key focus for the work done there.

This section of our process presumes that a leader with a group has crossed into liminal space, moving from the known to the unknown, or into disruption of beliefs and assumptions, all within a container that loosely holds the movement. We continue with the water metaphor, in its several forms, to describe the facets of liminal space and how they may arise in no particular order, affecting group interaction and personal wisdom. Ultimately through this journey, courage, experimentation and playfulness will manifest themselves as people learn to trust each other with both vulnerability and courage, as they tell their stories and dreams for the future – either in their places of work or in the wider trajectory of their lives.

"Powerful waters"
New Zealand, 2015

Chapter Four

FLOWING WATER

Encountering Change, Trusting the Process

A river creates her own patterns. She starts with a few drops of curiosity in one direction, followed by a trickle of play in another, and eventually the route is engraved for greater surges of creativity and streams of delight to follow.
– Eila Carrico[1]

I am a kayaker. I prefer the waters of a large lake that has some wave movement or a river with mild sets of rapids. The extreme sport videos of kayakers throwing themselves over the edges of waterfalls with rocks waiting to meet them at the bottom have no appeal for me. However, launching myself into waters unfamiliar can be exciting as long as I know that my boat can handle the currents and the waves. I have learned over time that, when moving through rapids or turbulence, I must keep paddling hard rather than merely letting the water do all the directional work. A few upsets with my boat showed me that water itself flows wherever it can and I have to do some work to move with it or else be overturned. In the midst of the journey, I must watch for hidden barriers, feel shifts in currents, anticipate my next moves and be ready for surprises. I also have to keep my center of gravity in the kayak. Sometimes I get wedged between rocks or get caught by a rogue wave and have to improvise to regain maneuverability. So it is with liminal space as we immerse in transitions, hopefully with helpful tools at hand.

This chapter dives deeply into encounters with the unknown, that which is different when immersed in the waters of liminal space. These encounters draw attention to questions of self-identity and the identities of others, in contexts of work, relationships, religions and sociopolitical realms.

Those who intentionally enter a space to foster change because they cannot or choose not to stay in the *status quo* may consider this process a mere short-term brainstorming or planning session. While dreaming and planning share some method with experience in liminal space (such as creating a future with ideas for an organization or a project with shared intention), they are not the same as the internal and relational work required for actual transformation in transition. Participating in liminal space requires that group members go deep into their own center, which often means leaving thought-based judgments or theories behind at the edges of this space. Experience and reflection upon experience (what one notices and to what one gives attention, not how one analyzes) are the primary foci for living in the flow of liminal space. Essential for movement in liminality is the willingness to encounter change, observe, stay centered, and trust flow, while using one's tools to work with, rather than against, movements arising.

We bring our own life-experiences into transitions; we automatically rely on what we know and pay attention to what has worked successfully for us in the past. We have particular beliefs about ourselves and others, including our roles and our sense of effectiveness in various areas of expertise or talent. At the same time, in liminal space these very beliefs may end up being our first barriers to working with the flow of transition. The more deeply beliefs are entrenched, the more likely they will keep us from moving forward effectively. Raising awareness about these deeply held convictions will be essential for powerful, positive change.

Chris Argyris, a Harvard University researcher in human organization and development, describes how we develop our belief systems through a particular mental process. His "Ladder of Inference," later used by Peter Senge in his now classic *The Fifth Discipline: The Art and Practice of the Learning Organization*,[2] is instructive. Argyris starts with a ladder metaphor, naming the bottom rung as observable data or information we gather with our senses. From what we sense, we select what we would like to attend to from our data based on what we deem relevant and discard the rest. From there, we make assumptions about what is important, ascribing meaning to them. At this point, we begin to conclude that our meaning-making is accurate and we can draw further conclusions about our assumptions as we make our way up the ladder. Finally, we develop a set of beliefs based on our initial awareness, often assuming that these beliefs are universal, and take action based on those beliefs as if they were facts. A loop is established on this ladder, because once our beliefs are in place, we pay attention to data that supports them and continue to ignore what seems irrelevant, thereby creating a semi-closed feedback or reflexive loop. This pattern of taking data and interpreting it, then using the interpretation as fact is very common in individuals and organizations and can lead to closed loops that no longer accept difference or diverse thought. We become trapped.

David Gray adapted Argyris's work to create a "Pyramid of Belief," similar to the ladder of inference with emphasis on a "bubble" of belief that serves to reinforce biases that we often call facts, often fiercely defended.[3] He starts with a baseline for the pyramid, which he calls "reality," an unknowable for human beings in any pure sense. We pay attention to certain parts of reality based on our experiences, which in turn determine where we focus our energy and further attention. Based on what human beings notice and attend to (need or want), we make theories about them based on selected facts that we notice. Once our theories are confirmed for us, we make judgments, often reinforced by people around us who have similar experiences and attentions. Finally, when judgments are reinforced long enough, we move into a belief system, which we tend to share with like-minded people, in a group

Gray calls "the obvious" or the "bubble of belief."[4] Further, belief systems defend themselves, especially when disrupted with another perspective.

Thus, to be in liminal space together, particularly with those who espouse different belief systems, we must recognize that we are not present to make a point of defending our identity and our territory. In fact, we might be wrong about some of our assumptions and the beliefs derived from our own mental frames. This commitment to openness is especially essential in diversity-based conversations. Race and gender relations, different physical and mental abilities, varied economic spheres, religious beliefs, approaches to global development and cultural norms all deeply affect the business, social and religious values we bring to the world. Approaching these conversations without an open mind blocks the imagination about co-creating a robust future that includes myriad populations.

Many businesses and nonprofit organizations have begun to address the benefits of diversity, both in terms of human representation in the company or organization and human thought processes themselves; disparate approaches to problems or innovations create a stronger product or service, meeting the needs of stakeholders much more effectively than a one-size-fits-all mindset. Such organizations seem to be ahead of most religious organizations in terms of valuing difference as a means of creating a stronger community of work and practice. McKinsey & Company, with presence in sixty-five countries, invests in private, public and social sectors to help create meaningful change through design and analysis of mindsets and processes.[5] The company claims, "Though our groundbreaking research, we have set out a compelling business and economic case for diversity. Using our global reach, we share our insights, convene partnerships for action, and serve clients to inform critical decision makers with the power to make real change."[6]

Forbes relates levels of diversity in a company to its financial success. There are four reasons diversity matters according to Grace Reyes, a Forbes Finance Council member: better financial performance – for every ten per cent in ethnic diversity rincreased in the senior executive team, earnings increase by roughly 0.8 percent; increased employee engagement where individuals understand they each have a voice; increased financial performance due to diversity, including intellectual diversity; and improved company reputation as the company provides goods and services to a wider span of populations.[7]

This recognition of the value of diversity allows for meaningful conversation that is broad and deep, no matter what the goal of the gathering or the context in which it occurs. Creating a container for liminal space invites people into the conversational milieu of their social or business culture so that identities and belief systems are brought to the surface, discussed and nuanced for positive, forward-moving impact. Once immersed, the challenges and disruptions to our own belief systems are difficult to ignore should we adopt learning-postures in this space.

However, socioeconomic differences seem to be moving in a different direction in the political sphere, especially during times of crisis. The motivation for unity in the midst of diversity has been trumped by a widespread desire for self-protection or self-gain, based on belief systems entrenched in fear and anger about the "other." The rise of violence via mass shootings or terrorist acts parallels the rise of anger that has defined "other" as "not me." This mass mental illness is entrenching in the United States and other countries throughout the world, where resentments run deep and polarization turns violent. This deep division worsens as fear rises about financial stability. The more polarized people become, the more likely societies get stuck. It is here that the most difficult work must be done and it can only be done in liminal space, where the container allows for suspension of judgment in one's own belief systems to be able to hear the "other." Reasoned, transparent thinking and calm voices are essential in crisis and in any moments of change in various social sectors. For example, addressing human social illness directly will affect those in the business world who desire to make moral decisions about their participation in profit-making that also focuses on the betterment of society, rather than turning a blind eye to its possible negative impacts or destructive tendencies.

Encountering New Spaces with Powerful Questions

Immersing in the flow while a facilitator-leader holds the container is not easy at first, particularly for those who prefer to focus primarily on systematic problem-solving, task lists and clear goals pointing toward clear outcomes. However, living this way for a time is essential for deep change, requiring uneasy suspension of the structures we often hold dear. Loosening our tight hold on our belief systems necessitates a "let's see what happens" or experimental mindset. If new beliefs arise, they can be tested by experience.

If we think of the ladder of inference process described briefly above, we see that work in liminal space begins to foster questions about what we pay attention to as we make observations about data. Powerful questions about our selection of what is important in the sensing stage, as well as our subsequent interpretations and assumptions, begin to raise awareness about how our belief systems are built in the first place. This work is difficult and often painful for people, especially when the beliefs are deep and have been established for decades. A good facilitator-leader or coach gauges the level of difficulty being experienced by an individual or group and gears questions toward the depth of disruption that is emerging. Thus, work in liminal space focuses on our selections about what is important, how we make meaning out of those choices, our assumptions and our conclusions. Beliefs and resulting actions become more visible and reflection on them becomes possible. The power of good questions makes this shift attainable at this point of immersion.

Many years ago I entered my own liminal space in an intense six-day immersion that was focused on learning more about US racial tensions among African Americans, European Americans and indigenous peoples.[8] I was very wary of what I might encounter in a small group of white people gathering to work on our own racism. I had had my awareness raised significantly in South Africa about the economic sources of a cultivated racism; I knew that the *status quo* could not stand. I also knew that I needed to do some internal work. Yet, was I ready to hear the stories I had not been taught in history class or encountered in my travels abroad? Could I handle rage leveled against me? How would I deal with my own shame of being part of the ongoing centuries of institutionalized slavery? Would I encounter white supremacists who thought it was their right to dominate and dehumanize, based on very different belief systems than mine? Prior to participation in the immersion, I recalled hearing someone saying very clearly that slavery never happened in the United States. Would I be meeting people living with this level of denial?

Suspending my fears also required that I suspend my foregone conclusions, my belief systems. I learned that white guilt was a hindrance to moving forward. I learned that rage was a crucial thing to receive from people who had the mark of centuries of slavery in their DNA. I learned that there are many forms of modern-day slavery still occurring all over the world, including in my own county. I learned that I had to claim my voice as a white woman to counter the hate-messages from other white people that reinforced polarization and domination. I heard stories about the devastating harm of the denial of slavery and the terrible dehumanization leading to violence, even genocide. I left the sobering immersive experience in deep pain, but I gave up my shame and I gave up my fear, as did many others in the room. Now I pay attention to the subtle inequalities that are everywhere for people of color; I ask my own questions about who is missing from the conversation or the curriculum and I pay attention to different voices in a new way, with greater respect and inquiry than I did in the past. "What's it like to . . ." are words that come into my conversations often now. Prior to this particular experience, I was prone to say, "I can relate . . .".

At the time of the liminal immersion, I had to learn to go with the flow of the water, which was held in a container by the teacher-facilitator, Melanie. Melanie laid out the acceptable way we were to communicate and the space where we could be vulnerable if we chose to be. Over time, she pushed us to give voice to our experiences and emotions. Only then did the participants begin to become deeply honest. The flow in that space took us on a fast, turbulent journey down the river. Sometimes we were stuck in the rocks, sometimes we did not paddle hard enough or at all. If we fought the currents, we became exhausted and weak. If we actively paddled with the current, though we hit some rocks and suffered some bruises, we sustained each other and found new ways forward, with new understanding of racial dynamics and our own bubbles of belief disrupted.

My experience is not unique. However, it is an example of how living in liminal space can lead to transformative encounters evoking alternative views and ways of being in the world. The components of working with the flow help reflection on belief systems and even can actively disrupt them.

Consciousness-raising

Once we enter the waters of liminal space, we must recalibrate balance because the flow is not moving at a pace or in a manner to which we are accustomed in our day-to-day experience. There are rocks and creatures below the surface we can't immediately sense, and we remain wide-eyed to take in the riverbank and the rocks to make sure we can find our way to safety if need be. Pressure gradients differ. Senses are more alert. Awareness heightens. The new experience invites us to notice what we haven't paid attention to before. If we submerge in the water and look up, we see completely different perspectives about what is above and around us. This experience creates either curiosity or dread about what is around the next bend. So, we use our tools.

Initially, we work on stabilizing ourselves so that we can manage the flow, avoiding as many hazards as possible. Over time, we begin to understand how this particular flow works and how we respond to it. When we get to this level of acceptance regarding flow, we are ready to explore our encounter with the water itself and where it might be taking us.

Travelers who eschew tour buses and are curious about engaging with other cultures have a sense of this working-with-the-flow. For example, if a person prefers a slower pace than a tour group and stays in one place long enough, she or he may have a bit of time in a coffee shop, tea-room or wine café. Most interesting is to hear the surrounding conversations.

They range from mundane routines to scandal to the great local epics, with a bit of gossip in the mix. Conversations about the events at the annual town picnic or the joy of a local girl or boy making it to a national-level sports competition or the angler who caught the largest fish on record, all reveal what matters to people. Each time a stranger is in their midst, the stranger and the local people change each other, perhaps just a little. Values and beliefs are conveyed through stories and they are clarified or disrupted through questions.

Liminal space, the space that is not our first home or dwelling place, but a transitional one, is where we suspend what is normal to us and jump into a new kind of flow. We learn things we didn't know. We suspend our own pre-judgments and widen our view to see what the river yields to us. In learning immersions, liminal space often results in consciousness-raising. Travelers who commit *not* to being in a group of people like themselve, who want to be in conversation with others not like them, experience this consciousness-raising more easily. Perspectives change, understanding deepens, barriers can be broken down if they exist, bridges crossed, adventure adopted and shared. Likewise, in crisis, we suspend our sense of normalcy and stabilize what we can, but are forced to widen our view for what might be forthcoming.

Consciousness-raising is inviting people to a deeper awareness, which means to hear and experience a point of view radically different to their own. It is meant to widen one's own worldview, based on the experiences of others that do not immediately resonate with one's own participation in life's events. In other words, one becomes conscious of a much wider perspective than one's own personal belief system.

Another important aspect of consciousness-raising is thinking through the implications of how we make others "other." This "othering" or alterity, the claim of being radically different to the point of alien, often carries judgments and stereotypes with it. For example, people of color know that when they enter a primarily white establishment for a meal or a shop to buy an item, they will be stared at as suspicion mounts. Often, they know they are being watched either covertly or overtly; the air crackles with alertness. Immediate "othering" stems from stereotyping. Consciousness-raising not only critiques this behavior in one's self, but also interrogates how this behavior came to be through the belief systems that become entrenched throughout our lives. In other words, consciousness-raising is not merely personal. It identifies systems that perpetuate discrimination and creates a lens of empathy and, it is to be hoped, solidarity for deep change.

Consciousness-raising calls for a rising awareness that habits and beliefs from the past no longer serve to bring about the best in us. New awareness is the gateway to moving well in the flow of change, which invites us to become curious and ask new kinds of questions. We wonder about the making of meaning and how we encounter meaning through different possibilities for the present and/or future.

To enter this expanded consciousness, we need to address what Arlie Russell Hochschild refers to as the "empathy wall," a wall or block that precludes us from attempting to connect with someone with different beliefs than ours. To bring this wall down, we must suspend our own entrenched belief systems, a difficult prospect when we feel challenged or under pressure. Hochschild puts it this way:

> The empathy wall is an obstacle to deep understanding of another person, one that can make us feel indifferent or hostile to those who hold different beliefs or whose childhood is rooted in different circumstances. In a period of political tumult, we grasp for quick certainties. We shoehorn information into ways we already think. We settle for knowing our opposite numbers from the outside.[9]

Hochschild goes on to question whether human beings can shift to see reality through someone else's eyes. Of course, such a shift requires a sense of not being under attack or a state of mind that is not inherently narcissistic. Ultimately, she asks us to climb the empathy wall by intentionally and deeply listening to stories dissimilar to our own, accompanied by the feelings within them.

This disruption, based on suspending one's own stereotypes, changes the way we work, converse and play together. Implicit bias training is one tool that many businesses, nonprofit organizations and some religious organizations have adopted to address stereotyping. Unfortunately, while much of the work does increase awareness, it is not developed further because the race conversation (as well as other conversations about gender, sex, ability and so forth) require long-term commitment and difficult inner work to mobilize enough energy for active change. Usually conflicts arise. If the facilitator-leader holding the container is capable of creating space for conflict to do its empowering work where people are deeply listened to, then conflict can serve a positive purpose. However, if a facilitator-leader is conflict-avoidant, the flow stops and people become stuck, or worse, polarized. If consciousness-raising stops at the instructional level through training and diversity initiatives designed to meet quotas, rather than moving into liminal, disruptive space, change is unlikely to occur. Instead, people claim that they now must be "politically correct," a thin disguise for resentment about being challenged at the belief-system level. Therefore, deepening the conversation is necessary for real change.

Finally, asking powerful questions is a primary way to evoke consciousness raising. The power of the good question stretches, even punctures, our bubbles of belief and pulls us into deeper awareness of our current assumptions and conclusions; it also invites us to examine how we arrived at them in the first place. Genuine curiosity about someone else or another group of people not like us generates questions for the sake of learning, of course with sensitivity to the behavioral norms of the culture in which one is asking. Curiosity also creates space for others to speak about their identities and choices on their own terms.

The power of a good question stretches, even punctures, our bubbles of belief and pulls us into deeper awareness of our current assumptions and conclusions; it also invites us to examine how we arrived at them in the first place. Genuine curiosity about someone else or another group of people not like us generates questions for the sake of learning, of course with sensitivity to the behavioral norms of the culture in which one is asking. Curiosity also creates space for others to speak about their identities and choices on their own terms.

How one asks a question is as important as what questions are asked; voice and body indicate support and interest, or the opposite. My training as a leadership coach involved learning the difference between effective and ineffective questioning for the purpose of raising awareness in a person or group. The idea is not to problem-solve or fix a situation, but to invite the conversation into awareness of the present moment.

Facilitative questions avoid interrogation, focusing less often on the "why" questions that attorneys, detectives, doctors, analysts, or researchers predominantly ask. Instead, the purpose is to elicit a person's belief systems, thoughts, meaning-making, or feelings without asking for justification or creating an opposing, rather than curious, stance.[10]

Of course, curiosity has room for the "why," though after an explanation is reached, there is possibility to go deeper in conversation about meaning-making ("how did you get there?" and "what is important in this belief or situation?"). Attending to discourse and non-verbal communication beyond "why" explanations moves the dialogue from gathering information to deeper understanding of values, behaviors, and beliefs. Potential for consciousness-raising about one's own bubbles of belief occurs alongside others' changing levels of self-awareness, thereby opening potential for expanding worldviews and deepening the conversation.

Deepening the Conversation

As I write this chapter, I am looking out of a large window overlooking a Nova Scotian harbor, watching the sea flow in and out every six hours or so. The tides, dependent on the gravitational pull of the moon, shift their times daily; high tide and low tide are approximately 45 minutes later each day as the tides circle around the human-created clock. Bird life and fish life move with this flow, back and forth through the harbor.

This steady ebb and flow, back and forth, has its own disruptions depending on the relative calmness or chaos of the weather. Higher tides can occur with storms during hurricane seasons. Add great surges of water from wind or earthquake, then high tide becomes deadly. Wildlife adjusts not only to water flow but to conditions traveling through the weather system. Sometimes seabirds simply sit on the water's surface and are propelled toward land or away from it as they rest on the tidal waves. Sea mammals and fish "read" the flow and adjust accordingly as they are able.

Liminal space has ebb and flow much like the tides. Individuals may experience this flow differently of course, but as a group, they may undergo great disruptions or breakthroughs and then a time of relative quietude, what I call "waiting expectantly." Going with the flow means noticing what is happening internally and also within the relationships in this space. Reading not only the movement but knowing where the container is what keeps people in tune with the nature of change in this space.

Deepening the conversation may require rest periods or it may require pushing hard if complacency arises in the group. Asking questions of oneself and of others based on the topic at hand and one's identity in it can keep the work "in the flow." On the other hand, retreating to one's comfort zone impedes movement; this retreating is not the same as resting for a moment. Even the birds in the tidal flows must rest. Resting usually involves reflection and self-care, especially when one has had a belief system up-ended, but with intent to return to dialogue and questions. One of the most powerful questions I know, "Who do we choose to be?", is triggered by Margaret Wheatley's assertion that identity in this "day and age, is manufactured to be self-promoting."[12]

To deepen the conversation about identity and beliefs, one might ask any individual, group, team or community, "How do our choices separate or connect us with life's meaning and purpose?" The answer to that particular question is to dive deeply into what meaning and purpose exist for the work ahead and the relationships that foster movement in that direction. The resulting conversation is most likely to be liminal in nature, crossing a threshold into a space of curiosity, learning, evolving identity-formation, and perhaps chaos for a time.

United Methodist Bishop Karen Oliveto in her book, *Together at the Table*, tells a story about a man in her former church, Glide Memorial in San Francisco, who attended a weekly "Speak Out" session where people spoke their own truths. This regular Wednesday night gathering was created to bring about deep listening and care for the identity of others:

> Each Wednesday, an amazing collection of humanity gathered: homeless and housed, addicts and those in recovery, sex workers and Glide staff, congregants and tourists came together to the tell the truth of their lives. One evening, a young man wove his way to the microphone and swayed in silence in front of us. His rotting teeth exposed the depth of his addiction. His glassy eyes and twitching body gave away the fact that he was quite high. The usual noise around the room settled the longer he stood in silence at the microphone. When the room was totally quiet and all eyes were upon him, he looked at us and said, "Can I trust you with my dignity?"[13]

Such a question disrupts us on many levels: stereotypes about who deserves our pronouncements on being dignified, willingness to listen to someone who is high, and our notions of "good" and "bad" in terms of how we define identity. Bishop Oliveto goes on to say that this man's question was seared into her soul, for he had delivered a sudden, strong, new perspective to her and to many in the room. This kind of disruption is what is necessary for transformation. It is a struggle, for letting others' stories and others' questions of us change how we define ourselves may require some surgery on our belief systems. This work can be done in a liminal space that has a facilitator who holds the container for us no matter how we navigate the flow.

Positives and Negatives

Liminal work in liminal space is complex work, requiring stamina and resilience. When we cannot sustain such complex learning, we find ourselves among others who buoy us. The group is present within a container to carry us for a while in the flow until we are ready to move again. While navigating the ebb and flow, as well as the currents, we begin to get a stronger sense of direction, perhaps for survival, but certainly for the movement toward transformation of self, group and environment.

It is difficult not knowing what lies around the bend of the river or what will be brought in with the tide, or even what will be left behind by it. This uncertainty and the very nature of in-between-ness may be deeply frightening to those who are used to clear parameters, demarcations, rules, titles denoting positional power and dogma. Certainty blurs, and some participants turn to micro-level details to regain a sense of control. Getting lost in the details of the discourse can lead a person to yearn for the "good old days" when things were perceived as simpler, where everyone one knew her or his "place." Granted, as non-dominant people seek liberation from stereotypes that predetermine roles in family and society, the world has become more complex in terms of negotiating roles for those who live in advantaged circumstances.. As it must be. However, this complexity is negative primarily for those who are in dominant positions in the public or private sectors, the work or home places. For others who have always struggled to break free of chains not of their own making, complexity has been a constant. The "good old days" were good for those in power, or for those who rode on the tails of this power. Liminal space with its momentum toward positive change is likely to threaten structures of power and privilege and this in turn always fosters a backlash to protect the powerful and privileged.

Liminal space is challenging space. Knowing the steadiness of the container, especially in the early days of the work, and trusting the facilitator are imperative when going with the flow. If one can trust, even if it takes time, then the fear or discomfort turns to a sense of inquiry into what adventure is unfolding in front of an individual or the group itself. The "good new days" are ahead for those willing to participate.

"Glacial movement"
Antarctica, 2007

Chapter Five

ICE

Standing Strong, Fostering Courage

The noise resembles the roar of heavy, distant surf. Standing on the stirring ice one can imagine it is disturbed by the breathing and tossing of a mighty giant below.
– Ernest Shackleton[1]

Ice that forms on bodies of water is indeed how Shackleton describes it: water continues to move beneath it, often unseen, and the ice constantly changes in its interaction with the air above it and the water below.

Ice that forms on land tells its own story. Being in the presence of a glacier is a phenomenal experience. Seeing a massive, thick sheet of blue and white ice working its way down mountains and slowly, surely, dragging with it whatever is in its path, invites respectful silence. In that silence, one can hear the sounds of cracking and shifting as the ice continues its descent, remaining solid and shifting at the same time. Eventually, the ice meets water or becomes a stream as it melts. When flowing into the oceans, the glacier calves into icebergs, sometimes suddenly and with explosive noise. Anyone standing on the shoreline during these events must walk swiftly to higher ground, for the water displaced by the new iceberg dropping into the sea becomes a wave that can wash away shore-dwellers.

Many glaciers are ancient; the most recent discovery claims the oldest is aged eight million years.[2] In our day and age, these glaciers are either buried and beginning to surface or moving quickly toward the sea. As ice caps melt and glaciers calve into icebergs free-floating on the seas, we are conscious of a world that is heating and melting. Before glaciers reach the sea, scientists can monitor the rate of flow over the land, depending on the temperature and pressure at their base.

Geologists know through ice-core samples that the most ancient ice carries within it air that has been trapped for millennia, making the normal translucent clear-white color blue. That's why Antarctica is called the Blue Continent. As glaciers move, they carry this ancient air and other solid debris with them until they melt, at which time the air escapes and the debris sinks to the earth floor or washes away in glacier-melt streams.

Leaders and Ice

Like ice, leaders find their work dependent on context. Pressures and flow speeds differ depending on time, space, demands and stakeholders. Leaders know that they need to be both flexible like water and, at times, grounded and directional like ice. Therefore, while leaders work with the flow in liminal space, we also may come to a place where we need to become like an ice floe. We continue to move, but we are not swayed in our core by whatever the river or sea surfaces in front of us. There are occasions to take solid stances that are not influenced by current trends, political voices or crises.

The story of Ernest Shackleton's second voyage to Antarctica illustrates this concept well, with literal ice involved, in this case endangering the lives of him and his crew.[3] In 1914, Shackleton, an Anglo-Irish explorer, left England to voyage to Antarctica on the *Endurance*. His ship became trapped in ice and drifted for ten months, then was crushed in pack ice. The crew survived and drifted on ice floes for five months, then used their small boats to escape to Elephant Island (South Shetland Islands), where they subsisted on sea mammals and birds. Taking five of his men, Shackleton left Elephant Island in one boat and sailed 800 miles to South Georgia over sixteen days in some of the roughest seas in the world. Four months later, in the year 1916, after several forays to rescue the remaining crew, Shackleton brought the remaining twenty-two men to safety. Few leaders could have done so.

What did Shackleton do to save all his men? As a leader, he first took a stance that they would live despite all odds. His stance was solid and clear to the men. Then he knew that he would have to foster the skill sets of each man in community with all the others, giving them meaningful tasks, rotating jobs to relieve boredom, initiating play to foster teamwork and camaraderie, and talking to each crew member individually and supportively as the men dealt with their situation. He kept a routine and a hierarchy where every member of his crew was valued and respected but he clearly was in charge (he created a container). He spent time alone listening to the ice and analyzing daily what the ice and the weather would bring. Fortunately, he had hired a second-in-command who exhibited resilience and goodwill and so was able to trust that there was another to keep the container stable. Finally, he weighed the risks of taking a boat through wild seas to try and find help, and then set out on a horrific journey with a handful of malnourished men. We know that the ending was positive, but the story itself was liminal space thrust upon the crew in the most extreme conditions possible. They lived to tell the tale of a real heroes' journey that almost sounds superhuman.

Hence, in liminal space, we live in paradox. Shackleton knew that he had to keep his eye on the future and that he was going to rescue his men. At the same time, he had to work with daily conditions and minimal resources. He paid attention to the details of the day and stayed true to his stance through the skills and fortitude he already had. Similarly, we work to flow with the current and at the same time stay solidly grounded in our deepest knowing. This deep knowing exists beyond our formed belief systems and stems from the collective unconscious.[4] In other words, groundedness does not constitute an opinion or political stance, but a sense that we have a unique contribution to make to the planet that is deeply powerful and called for in light of the world around us. No one can take this groundedness or center from us. This deep knowing does not alienate others because its motive is always to move toward healthy relationship, which some would call "love," playing out in myriad ways among the planet's living beings. With this motive, we stand steady, even if we are asked to move in the opposite direction from our convictions, about decisions that are life-giving rather than self-serving. This collective unconscious, available to all beings, avoids divide-and-conquer tactics for personal gain. Our belief systems and worldviews may transition regarding the method for powerful, positive change, even if in the midst of crisis, but the core intention to bring life-giving connections to the planet stays solid even in the midst of flow.

Where We Go and What We Carry

As rivers flow along boundaries of soil or rock and seas constantly sculpt shorelines, they carve new pathways that have not existed before. Some of the carving is predictable based on currents, trajectories, inclines and composition of rock and sand. Some depends on unknown factors such as unusual rises and falls in water level, storms, droughts and influences of the other elements – air (wind), fire and earth. When ice moves, it also follows the path of its boundaries, though far more slowly, because it is water in another form. It follows the currents, melting and eventually becoming or joining the water that carries it. Until that time, ice holds substances inside its shape. Sometimes these substances include rocks, dirt, leaves, bones, debris or anything ice has encountered or picked up on its journey.

Similarly, when we take stances and hold firm, we carry with us our past, our families' pasts and a great deal of the messaging we have learned from the worlds around us. We carry our cultures, our beliefs and our experiences and we are prone to defend them by surrounding them with protective boundaries. In short, we carry the content and experiences of our lives with us, and, in most cases, the generations of lives that have shaped us, wherever we go. Ice is permeable or it wouldn't pick up rocks, soil and other solids that stand in its path. As it melts, it yields these things to the water or the earth. As we open up, we yield our stories and offer them to those with us in liminal space.

There is a time in every journey when we also need to hold firm. We might be responding to an emergency with expertise while everyone else is panicking. Or perhaps someone pushes hard against our own beliefs that we have spent a great deal of time constructing with an open mind and lots of listening. Perhaps someone else has determined that we are wrong and she or he is right. Or perhaps we have more information than we have divulged and so suggestions or questions from others do not make sense to us. Rather than dissolving our own center into the flow of everyone else, we ride with them without melting. We honor what we know in our core to be true while still moving slowly and with intention as needed, respecting the differences around us and picking up new information and experience along the way.

This principle is particularly important in the business world, where agility and pace are points of much discussion. Both corporations and small businesses know that the market changes not only with each generation but with trends that can catch on like wildfire. At the same time, I hear people in their midlife and older years lamenting that very few products are as reliable as they once were. A friend recently was encouraged by those with long-term expertise about appliances to have her 35-year-old washing machine repaired rather than purchase a new one. Planned obsolescence or simply cheap products have effectively limited or removed the choices for consumers, many of whom crave reliability and long-term use. Appliances, electronics, cars, houses and heavy machinery all fall into this category and the manufacturing and design worlds are caught between producing the "latest and greatest" products and the call for reliability and long-term quality.

Standing firm while embracing innovation requires traversing a fine line. For example, I have noticed that automobile commercials these days emphasize the safety and quality of their vehicles at the same time as attempting to paint a picture of new adventure or social connection. I no longer see advertisements with the presumed sales enticement of thin, scantily-clad women draping themselves across cars that are bought by men; instead the emphasis is on either speed and success for women or men (the consistent message adopted for luxury cars) or safety and adventure for groups of friends or families, whether traditional or non-traditional (steadfast mid-range models). Each comes with a message of reliability while targeting potential customers based on current values, experiences, identities and lifestyles.

Individual leaders also encounter this fine line between standing firm and opening to the rapid flow of change as they hold the possibilities of the future, current capabilities and what worked in the past in their lines of sight. Holding all of these aspects simultaneously means living with paradox – fast and slow must exist together; they should not be separate approaches. In the paradox, there are embedded poles. Managing this fine line between the polarities of fast-invention for quick production and slow-experiment for time to test reliability requires attention to the positive and negative aspects of each approach.

To continue with our automobile example, we see the trend that is now a movement rather than a fad: fuel-efficient, hybrid vehicles. It is apparent that this market for fuel-efficiency will not go away because of concerns about natural resource (oil) availability, pricing and market fluctuations. Early adapters have been driving hybrid cars since 1999.[5] Now, every major manufacturer has a line of hybrid vehicles, with promises that most of their products will have a hybrid option soon. Honda and Toyota created the mass market by adapting hybrid engines long in existence to values and lifestyles of the public. Since then, with attention to economic trends in the world market regarding increased car usage, oil pricing and human preferences, companies have continued to develop the cars' reliability and update capabilities. Initial experimentation that took a hybrid car to mass market took risk within reason (flow with change, within a container). Standing firm with a product over time, despite initially low, and sometimes unsuccessful, sales from even earlier models of electric and hybrid cars, has created a market for electric and hybrid cars that is here to stay. Leaders who manage pace and commitment to quality foster sustainable progress. For example, in electric vehicles, batteries are on the brink of becoming recyclable, which signals a new opportunity for both the power sector and for the automobile industry in their ongoing commitment to decreasing dependency on the oil industry, lowering expense for the consumer by 2030 and integrating renewable energy into power grids.[6]

The same management of self holds true for our deep internal knowing about what relationships and values are life-giving – and what are not. We may have stances about issues very important to us and we also may be able to hear another point of view. Ultimately, we choose, in an informed way, and hold our center for ourselves, not necessarily because we've always thought this way, but because we have examined our own worldview in light of hearing others' experiences and stories and drawn conclusions for ourselves. Beliefs can change. Examined beliefs, ones that take into account external data and experience (the things we carry combined with the things we encounter), also can stay solid. We hold our stance, like ice, but that does not mean that we are not moving or that we may not melt and yield the matters that lie within. The difference between unexamined and examined belief systems is the level of awareness about how these stances have developed in the first place.

Mahatma Gandhi[7] shows us how to keep a clear stance based on examined beliefs. While living and studying in South Africa, Gandhi formulated his stance on justice as a way of protesting against race-based maltreatment of people of Indian origin, including a tax levied to keep them in indentured service status. There he organized a strike and protest march against the government tax. After his own imprisonment and upon return to his native India, Gandhi joined the Indian National Congress which was seeking Indian independence from British rule and soon became involved in the protest movement. On the day after the Amritsar Massacre of 13 April 1919 when British soldiers fired on a mass gathering of Sikh and Hindu people, killing 400 and injuring 1,000, Gandhi did not criticize the British. Instead he criticized his fellow countrymen for not exclusively using love to deal with the hate of the British government.

He challenged laws non-violently, urging people not to do business with the British. His heart stood in solidarity with the common people as he confronted the tyranny of leaders who ignored the plight of the poor. From his patient observations, relationships and experience, Gandhi formulated his stance. From there, he began to challenge the harmful policies of the British-ruled government for India. Even with calls for independence, he was concerned that India would replace one political system of leaders with another that had the same self-focus; the result would not change the economic disparity in his country. There had to be an alternative for the sake of the greater good.

Gandhi's speeches focused on non-violent, though not passive, resistance. He called for Indians to refuse to take part in systems that caused harm without breaking the law. For this stance, he was imprisoned more than once for sedition. Managing the polarity of resistance and respect for the law, Gandhi began to gain traction because people were hearing a quiet conviction about justice for all. Gandhi articulated an alternative in ways that captured people's hearts at the root of their being, a radical alternative.[8] In 1948, approximately six months after India gained independence, he was assassinated by a Hindu extremist. Gandhi, who dedicated his life to radical change through non-violent protest, is recognised as one of the most influential figures in the past two centuries. Notably, Martin Luther King, Jr studied and adapted Gandhi's approach during the civil rights movement in the United States.

When we pay attention to the roots of our being, collective unconscious combined with examined beliefs, we then become aware of an emerging vision that has meaning and purpose, unfaltering in the swift current of change. We stand. We continue to learn, but we do not follow every breaking trend or breath of wind.

Brave Space

As we have discussed, dwelling in liminal space takes courage. Flowing down the river or with the tides of the ocean takes a willingness to let go of the shoreline. Brave space is not necessarily the safe space we all wish we had on a regular basis. Brave space is risky even if there is a container to hold it steady for us as we move. Courage manifests itself when we are asked to state our views and, more deeply, how our views came into being in the first place, with room to be asked questions about our assumptions and stereotypes. We may need to apologize to people we offend. We may need not to apologize for standing strong. Bravery looks different for each person, depending on her or his sense of fear or weakness.

Only when vulnerability is expressed bravely and accepted as the gift that it is do the words "safe space" emerge. Participants then name their own points of connection and departure from the beliefs of the other members of the group. Other than beliefs that cause harm, the group in brave space can begin to broaden personal perspectives and move to deeper dialogue about the future. This opportunity is available for organizational teams who seek common purpose, religious communities and informal relationships.

Having made a case for standing firm while still allowing for flow, I want to add some additional complexity to the immersion in liminal space. There is more to this notion of paradoxical flow and stability and its management than deep knowing and standing firm. What we carry with us, in terms of our examined beliefs and subsequent action, when we manage to hold flow and focused stance together is a source of resilience in a world of constant change. Robert E. Quinn in *Deep Change* gives an example of the need for focus if organizational resilience is to be realized:

> Not long ago, securing a position in a large corporation meant life-long job security. This is no longer true. In today's world of hyper-change, organizations face more challenge and more uncertainty than ever before. Organizational members often find themselves feeling isolated, detached, and insecure. They crave a clear vision. What they are actually encountering however, is a continuous change and differentiation.[9]

This continuous change may or may not be liminal in its nature. If there is no end in sight, and the change itself is the constant, then there are no boundaries around it. There is nothing to hold onto, no anchor, no potential for equilibrium. To create a foundation in the midst of change we need a stance, a solid platform upon which to stop, look around and ascertain how to navigate forward to the next equilibrium. Quinn goes on to discusses how vision statements do not necessarily provide this foundation for corporations, and, I would add, any organization, until a powerful question is posed: "Who is willing to die for this vision?"[10] Who is willing to stand strong, with courage for this purpose?

Quinn has spent considerable time with companies that are floundering. He asked this very question to a group of executives after they had spent weeks of work dedicated to crafting a vision statement and presenting it to him for feedback. No one responded. What happened? The vision had become so general, so compromised, that no one could object. However, having no objections also fosters meaninglessness and, therefore, lack of inspiration or solid conviction about purpose.

Creating a collective, well-examined stance for an organization in the midst of change requires paying attention to the experience of employees, stakeholders as well as the executive team. There is a spiraling quality to creating awareness and choosing what is meaningful in these kinds of situations. In a healthy organization, input from the bottom and middle of the hierarchy influences the perspective at the top. The top of the hierarchy then articulates and implements a vision based on the attention given to input. Quinn calls this process paying attention to the "inner voice of the organization."[11] In unhealthy organizations, this process is unlikely to yield a vision that motivates others. People at the top of the organization are threatened by listening to voices that may offer criticism or critique. Therefore, the vision remains meaningless and self-serving, which means people work harder and harder for less effective results, breeding a spiral of lower satisfaction over time. In healthy organizations, the willingness to enter into a container with purpose but without predetermined outcome, to make space for powerful questions and to hold commitments that are core to the work, manages difference and allows emergence of a vision that matters.

Creating "brave space" rather than assuming "safe space" is becoming the focus of dialogues attending to diversity, equity, and inclusion (DEI), in the twenty-first century. The notion of cultural melting pots, where different people tolerate each other and focus on creating commonalities to minimize difference, has yielded to embracing difference as a preferable way for those whose values call for equity to be in the world. Such a preference requires finding a particular kind of courage to change by adopting a learning posture *and* holding a respectful stance in the midst of differences, some completely foreign. Brave leaders show courage when they do not shy away from difficulty or challenge and they show vulnerability when they are secure enough to admit mistakes.

Brené Brown has spent two decades studying the significance of vulnerability and courage in both individuals and the workforce and invites leaders to "live into" our values by managing vulnerability and courage. Based on her research conclusions, she puts these two behaviors together nicely as two facets of the same coin:

> The level of courage in an organization is the absolute best predictor of that organization's ability to be successful in terms of its culture, to develop leaders, and to meet its mission.
>
> The greatest challenge in developing brave leaders is helping them acknowledge and answer their personal call to courage. Courage can be learned if we're willing to put down our armor and pick up the shared language, tools, and skills we need for rumbling with vulnerability, living into our values, braving trust, and learning to rise. We fail the minute we let someone else define success for us.[12]

Brown took her observations to a United States Air Force base, Google and Pixar, among other organizations, all of which changed their outlooks based on the call for openness and bravery, or the courage to be vulnerable and still stand strong.

Some of the best leaders I have met personally embody this paradox of vulnerability and strength. One such woman, Toni, served as a consultant to my workplace upon my invitation.[13] Toni has many years of experience in academic administration and high-level diversity education. She serves on the faculty of a university that has an ethic of not only inclusion, but also welcome for people from all social locations.

Toni impressed me immensely in the way that met people of different ranks in the educational system exactly where they were, when attending to the agreed-upon agenda at my graduate school. She asked powerful questions, met challenges kindly and when, she was confronted with racism or sexism, her eyes would sparkle. I watched her energy rise as she began to ask the commentator before her very particular questions about values and beliefs, where these things originated and what experiences backed them up. In essence, she moved into the liminal work of the ladder of inference without naming it as such. She did not have to draw a line in the sand, become defensive or state her stance. Her questions made her values clear. She also was vulnerable enough to accept the answers of others without alienating them, accepting that she and they were in difference places. Even in high-tension situations, I could see that she was well-practiced and non-anxious in inviting others to reconsider their own unexamined stances. By the time she left the consultancy work with us after eighteen months, faculty wanted to hire her, students wanted to take classes with her and I wanted her as an on-campus colleague. Toni continues her work at her university of choice, making a significant difference in the trajectory of many lives there, both vulnerable and courageous, creating brave space as a container wherever she goes.

Unintentional Emergence

Calling forth brave space does not always progress as well as with Toni. There are frequent complications. We return to our metaphor once again. As a glacier gathers debris while it moves downhill, and as an iceberg follows the current of the ocean or lake into which it falls, they continue to gather and release material. In liminal space, vulnerable and potentially disruptive as it is, we can expect that belief systems will be challenged and surprises arise from what we carry with us or what we experience around us. These tensions in us can cause tension in the conversational dynamic. A facilitator will be prepared to manage the container when intense feelings come forth. Here, the danger of polarization, as opposed to managing polarities, presents itself as people entrench to protect themselves or become ice-like about their ideas. Polarization is a movement that spreads like a pandemic virus. Once people see that lines are being drawn, they choose sides or choose to walk away.

There are two distinctions that need to be made about living within the tensions of liminal space. First, polarization needs to be distinguished from the tension of opposites. Living within tension on a spectrum where there are two poles does not mean we must live on the poles; we are not polarized.[14] A spectrum is a range of options, colors, feelings, behaviors, survey rankings or results that have a pole at each end. For example, when I was five years old, I learned that colors exist on a spectrum: ROYGBIV![15] Red existed on the hot side on one end and violet existed on the cold side on the other end, with the other colors of the rainbow in the middle. I was particularly enamored with green in the middle because it touched both blue and yellow and turned out to be a combination of the two.

Then things became complex when I learned in school that white was the presence of all colors and black the absence; this assertion didn't make sense to me. I couldn't figure out what the teacher was talking about. When I put all these colors from my paintbox together on paper, I made black! Not until I understood the principles of light refraction could I differentiate between solid colors and the workings of light. My original understanding had been expanded and I could differentiate between circumstances as I gained more information, understanding that context determined what made most sense.

In a brave space, or in a container that holds us well, we find our way into the tension and hold each of the poles steady from our perspective at the time. We are invited to meet in the middle of the tension, the green space on the color spectrum, if you will, and we see what kind of territory is there. We ask questions: what works for one person coming from one pole and what works for another coming from the other direction?

What is positive and negative about each? Or we might ask ourselves about our own extreme opinions on particular topics or in specific relationships. The conversation turns to managing the tension rather than living on the poles.

A second distinction is more subtle. Living within the tension is not necessarily living with paradox, although ironically, paradox always exhibits its own tension. Paradox occurs when two opposites are held together in the same space. In contrast, tension on the spectrum can have place with both ends, but it doesn't share its entire space with both. In time, when one is nearing the new equilibrium on the far edge of liminal space, living in paradox, complete with a particular tension of balancing two disparate things, may be its own equilibrium. However, while traversing the change itself, tensions must be navigated between this and that pole.

Natural tensions arise when worldviews are extremely polarized or when crisis arises. Those who live somewhere in the middle of the spectrum feel the tensions most acutely because they have access to both sides. For example, some people live between the poles of alienation and connection. In other words, one group of people would rather isolate themselves to be with those just like them and keep others out by building walls and barriers; and, at the opposite end, others work hard to keep relationships open and inclusive with few barriers at all. Most people live in the middle – some barriers seem necessary and some unnecessary. Liminal space allows for powerful questions about what is meaningful about our stances and how we learn to live in the tension, managing it with a sense of integrity and compassion.

Another tension arises when people encounter the poles of judgment and forgiveness. For some, judgment is a rule-based sense of accountability. Punishment is the only way to make amends, to even the score. The opposite extreme calls for forgiveness for all wrongdoing without attending to remorse, change and reconciliation. Many say, "It depends." Again, circumstances matter, creating a tension between two sets of beliefs. Taking context into account allows for managing the tension as well as possible. For example, the classic debate about how to respond to a person who robs a food store illustrates this tension well. The robber is arrested and brought to trial. The jury hears from one attorney that she broke the law and needs to be punished. The other attorney reveals that this woman is a mother of two children, just lost her job, has reached her allotment on food stamps and with soup kitchens and hasn't enough money to pay rent and buy food; she has to choose between homelessness and malnutrition, if not starvation. Jury members must make decisions based on their beliefs about the rules and compassion. Can they or the judge find a compromise? Or perhaps they can find something different: a Third Way.

A THIRD WAY

Sometimes in the midst of this living between poles, moving as we do, new understandings of the potential future emerge. A Third Way of thinking evolves. The linear spectrum is no longer deemed necessary and people jump off it altogether into a different, perhaps more complex view of the world. The COVID-19 pandemic has created a path for just this kind of evolution, the results of which remain to be seen. This Third Way, or a way different than the norm of creating a spectrum, sometimes is expressed by the term "intersectionality," coined in 1989 by Kimberlé Williams Crenshaw, a black feminist law professor. Intersectionality became a way of critiquing how discrimination arises based on a category: race, sex, age, economic status or ability.[16] Things get complicated when discrimination has overlapping categories of identity. Attention to the intersections of identity in the midst of our relationships and our work move us out of being somewhere on a spectrum (of age, status, ability, racialization or gender), getting us "outside the box" in terms of beliefs, relationships, and ways to create connection, as my students used to say.

Paying attention to the intersections of what makes the self, in addition to the complexity of values at the table of other selves, helps leaders understand that there is a complex web of connections that make up a person's identity, a team's perspective or an organization's leaders and stakeholders. Tension therefore is normal, expected and, if managed well, helpful. Welcoming discussion of intersections making up belief systems, values, perspectives and experiences has potential for tremendous creativity that also respects difference and diversity.

Tension may be an unintentional occurrence in liminal space unless the facilitator is savvy enough to remind the group that in liminality, these kinds of stresses are normal parts of the expansion of our minds and spirits. It hurts to stretch when muscles haven't been used for a long time. Likewise, it hurts to stretch our minds beyond the grooves they have inhabited for a long time. In fact, there may be some real grief involved as people have to let go of a lot of debris as they travel on the liminal path. In times of global crisis, we all experience some level of trauma whether directly affected by death or not. Even facilitators must find spaces to relieve some of the pain. The intensity of what we carry individually and as community may be of a magnitude that counseling or speaking with an expert is called for, so that that which hurts can be cared for in a proper, gentle and professional manner. Personal liminality comes into play even more forthrightly in these situations; dealing with past or present disruption pulls us into a journey of its own as we face our future.

The group moving in liminal space, if facilitated well, will be able to absorb the debris which we carry with some empathy. Icebergs may knock against each other but we are in the same flow. Naming our values and our experiences may not mesh with others'. However, an intellectual debate is not what this work is about. Neither is dismissal or an insistence on being right. The work requires courageous openness to flow and commitment to one's core values as the future unfolds.

The Collective Unconscious

To invoke Carl Jung, once again,[17] I find that the more I study, the more I believe that the collective unconscious plays a role in social movements on local and global scales. Social movements affect markets, religions, education and politics as values and desires shift and change; we see everywhere the intersection of differences among cultures and disagreements about what matters among generations. As we evolve in the modern/postmodern age, we also carry with us the wisdom of the ancient ways, ungirding our differences with a deep, common thread. Intersectionality matters, as does our common humanity.

Those living in liminal space are in prime position to attune to what is happening in the world around them as well as within. Suspending belief systems and stereotypes opens a level of observation and participation in the evolving dynamics of what Jung might call spiritual knowing and formation on a long-term, large scale. Furthermore, tapping into the archetypal stories Jung studied helps us to understand our own journeys thus far as part of a larger, ancient human movement with particular parameters that have existed for eons. Insights like this help us understand our own center and direct our attention to underlying meaning in the chaos of daily living. Here is where we hold firm because we are part of something much more ancient and much larger than we have been taught during our short lifetime.

In the early twentieth century, Jung proposed that there are archaic vestiges in the human psyche to which we still have access: "Jung held it to be the business of the psychologist to investigate the collective unconscious and the functional units of which it is composed – the archetypes, as he eventually called them."[18] These archetypes are what Jung described as psychic structures available to everyone as our common human heritage. Archetypes can be explored through mythology or through more recent studies that name normative behavior of leaders or learning and leadership style inventories.[19]

For Jung, the role of personal experience, in all its intersections, was to raise awareness of what is already present in us at our core, which he called the Self. Stevens summarizes Jung's assertion: "Our psyches are not simply a product of experience, any more than our bodies are merely the product of what we eat."[20] So, there exists in us common ground that is above and beyond experience or phenomena in a general sense, but human beings manifest this commonality in unique ways. For example, we recognize the human voice as held in common but each voice has a quality of sound-print that is different than all others throughout time. Jung attempted to prove his hypothesis by illustrating how different people throughout the world who had no knowledge of each other had very similar dreams. He also described an incident where a man dreamt about an image and its meaning that was almost identical to a mythological story from thousands of years ago, a story to which the man had had no access.

The significance of this theory based on Jung's observations is that there is indeed a core in all of us, which he would claim is a repertoire of behavior available to us, built into our structure as we have evolved as a species. This behavior is triggered innately when a particular stimulus occurs, based on a blueprint carried through generations and available at the time of birth.[21] Different behaviors become patterns as they are reinforced throughout time. We recall that, when in immediate danger, we normally react in one of three ways: fight, flight or freeze. These reactions are not initially taught, though they can be overridden with practice. Today, many fields of thought rely on the study of innate response patterns without reference to Carl Jung, including sociobiology, linguistics, ethnobiology and psychobiology.

Positives and Negatives

We can see unintentional awareness rising from traversing liminal space when the space is used for deep questioning and potential deep change. A Third Way or a different way forward can emerge, surprising participants and opening the door to an alternative future. A deeper sense of collective knowing can connect people involved in relationship – team, family, organization or simply the voices in one's head! The most significant element here is the ability to live in paradox: flow in a well-facilitated container that holds direction and purpose and, at the same time, hold one's well-examined stance. The collective unconscious brings the wisdom of time into conversation with current identity and experience and all its intersections.

The benefit of examining how one's beliefs have evolved is essential for our positive growth, both individually and in our personal and professional relationships. Our identity stems from our belief system and from the intersections creating us as a human being, alongside a deeper knowing, the collective unconscious. From these sources of our constitution, inherited and experienced (nature and nurture), we develop our wisdom, our connection to the collective heritage over eons and a sense of meaningful and unique purpose today. Learning to hold steady with this deep knowing while paradoxically staying open to change that moves us to our best self, and invites others to theirs, is an essential component of dwelling well in liminal space. Like the qualities of ice, we carve new paths through the surroundings we encounter while carrying the ancient wisdom with us. We are grounded while we are moving. We know what we carry with us. We are self-aware. We intersect with others' values and experiences while we know that we hold a common thread from ancient days.

There are also dangers in this space when we hold our stance. Self-examination is a life-long endeavor. There are particular times or topics for which self-examination can seem too threatening to our own egos or to the health of the group or team dynamic. When tensions are not well-managed, they tend to escalate, as people have different toleration levels for tension and respond differently to escalation. Some opt out of the conversation or plan altogether. Some become reserved and watchful, feeling unsafe. Some try to control the tension by dismissing it or taking command of the situation with decrees rather than questions. In the final case, holding a stance becomes a way to control rather than a way to remain true to one's values. People are easily swept off-balance to the point where they don't recover. The chaos becomes unmanageable and the open conversation grinds to a halt, usually with one or two persons pushing an agenda from their point of view. This flood of control lends itself to everyone else scrambling for safety elsewhere and the positive use of container breaks down.

Liminal space has tremendous potential to create powerful, positive change. However, the territory one must traverse is messy and confusing. In the midst of what feels like chaos, like an inexperienced person going white-water rafting on a level five river, a good guide can keep the raft afloat among the rocks and the currents. The guide or the facilitator knows that a deep and ancient undercurrent flows steadily under the chaos. Like the undercurrent, this flow is one that connects brain and heart to each other and all to others, producing a steadiness in the face of chaos, a stance that moves intentionally, deliberately and with purpose.

"Hot springs and mud pots"
Iceland, 2008

Chapter Six

STEAM

Setting Potential Free

Steam will always rise to the occasion.
– Anthony T. Hincks[1]

In middle school, I became enamored with earth science experiments thanks to a teacher with an adventuresome personality. We regularly made a tremendous mess in the science room. I realized in senior high that the best part of that particular course in earth science was that the teacher made us think about theories and then test them. Failure meant re-testing and changing our hypotheses. My teacher taught me how to think for myself through experiment and failure, fortitude and eventual celebration of success. Since eighth grade, I have been fascinated by scientific experimentation based on theoretical curiosity that needed some form of proof. Thus, when I entered the high school physics contest, I solicited my father for ideas about creating the most interesting experiment the judges had ever seen from someone my age. I trusted his creativity and I knew he would figure out something that connected with the earth sciences, based on his love of wood working and the outdoors. We played with ideas and he suggested testing the tensile strength of various types of wood. To do so, we chose five different one-foot long strips of wood with different densities and set each over the rim of a pot of boiling water for a set amount of time. At the end of the allotted time, we measured the malleability of each strip. I wrote my report, including the significance of the experiment, and won the contest. To this day, I know the particular fragrance of those five kinds of wood. I also discovered the power of water vapor that has turned to steam.

Steam is the most unrestrained, ethereal state of the configurations of water – the opposite of ice. It forms when there is pressure and heat, changing the density of the hydrogen and oxygen molecules so that water turns to gas. Its flow naturally rises unless it is contained in particular rooms, pipes or vessels for purposes of heating or cleansing. If left free, steam finds its way on air currents and combines with what already exists in the air. Before steam forms, water changes into vapor, which we can still see as droplets or mist. Steam itself is invisible to the naked eye but we can feel its heat and its movement.

Traversing through liminal space is like moving through unknown water, encountering water's three facets along the way. Flow of liquid mingled with steadiness of ice bring us two ways of living in this space. A way of moving forward from the container is shown by steam as it begins to rise from our creative journey, aiming at a new equilibrium. Steam not only results from the pressures and tensions found in liminal space but it also yields a new kind of freedom, a focus on potential and scenarios to develop into new possibilities for the future, whether a plan for new connections, new products, new organizational structures, new markets or simply a new way of being in the world. This freedom can come incrementally with small breakthroughs during the change process or in one big "aha" that leads directly to planning and implementation.

The Container Loosens

During the flow of work in liminal space, a facilitator has maintained a container so that the flow is not overwhelmingly chaotic or destructive. A measure of security is held so that the disruptive ideas and challenges are not altogether without boundaries. When participants have been in the flow for sufficient time to understand the boundaries and the movements involved, they themselves relax into the rituals of the contained space. Having done so, people find it easier to reveal vulnerable parts of themselves and express with each other emotion that they might not normally express. They are often able to disagree without entrenching, polarizing or arguing for the correctness of their claims. This relaxing into the space loosens the need for the facilitator to hold the container on her or his own. The group begins to do this holding and, at times, introduces variations. Ideally, the facilitator opens and closes the meeting or gathering and the participants create their own path through the agenda or discussion.

In the late 1980s during my early experience as a formal facilitator for an adult group, I held a container for a small group of women who found that their spiritual lives were adrift.[2] They were not being fed by religious institutions or various educational or self-help workshops they had attended. We agreed to gather for six months on a weekly basis and then assess what the way forward would be for the group. As we grew to know each other, the women found they were not only increasingly vulnerable about all aspects of their lives; they could also name their fears about their relationships, finances and the wave of politics that focused on hate. As they grew comfortable with the container and the ritual therein (we would light a candle and speak of the state of our soul at each gathering), the women began to contribute to the ritual with their own small additions. One said, "I would like to add to our conversation as we open the group. It would be helpful to hear a comment about where we each saw beauty in our stressful day." We added it. Another time, one woman wanted to know what random acts of kindness we had experienced that week. We added it. Still another requested that we bring a reading that most significantly impacted us in the last few years.

By the fourth month, the group turned to me and told me that they thought I should add something that was meaningful to me for the next ritual. At that point, I knew that, as facilitator, I was part of the group, still holding the container, but very loosely as they began to take responsibility not only for their own work, but also for the dynamics of the group in terms of sharing power and accountability. They were leading each other, together, while holding their parts of the container faithfully.

Since that time over the past three decades, I have facilitated mutual learning in many groups and teams, employing variations of the container. In every case, eventually including my approach to teaching in the academic classroom, the response has been similar to my 1980s experience. Participants, whether in interest groups or in teams working toward a particular purpose, would eventually foster enough courage to be vulnerable, to take stances based on their core values and to adopt learning postures. Further, in every case there were moments of "aha" where an idea was formulated, refined, thought through and, in the case of teams working on scenarios, plans developed. This Third Way, discussed briefly in Chapter Five, energized the participants into new ways of problem-solving or scenario-building to create a different kind of future. The *status quo* was on its way out and the future was beginning to unfold. They could feel the change even when it was not entirely clear to them what the new equilibrium would be like – yet.

Groups that gather for a purpose but without a prescribed outcome find that, in liminal space, there is possibility for creative re-creation. They discover what their stories mean for each other's worldview and they also find a way forward to make a difference in a hurting world. The woman's group from the 1980s created a domestic violence response program for churches in the area and carried out numerous training and advocacy events in the city. Living in liminal space together for six months opened doors they never imagined. Their stories, while quite different, eventually tuned into the concern they all cared about, finding common ground in the midst of different worldviews and even politics that normally would be considered at odds with each other. They discovered each other. Conversations included significant differences that were important because they were part of each woman's inner core, but these differences were not ultimately what mattered over time regarding their work in solidarity with victims and survivors of domestic violence. Tragically, at the end of our six months, one of our number was shot and killed by her fiancé in a domestic dispute. The shock led to a new layer and quality of liminal space for all of us as we gathered in outrage and grief to reconfigure our responses to her adult children, the press, the congregation and our own futures and actions. We hadn't seen the signs and we thought we were educated. We had to go back to our bubble of belief and examine ourselves again.

Once the participants in an intentional group take responsibility for their own journey and begin to care about others, they participate much more deeply in the flow. The container loosens as a generative spirit emerges. If the unexpected arises, sometimes in the form of tragedy, support and solidarity are available. Self-examination and investigation of ideas begin to tumble forth in conversation. Energy heightens. Deep knowing is less frightening. Of course, this dynamic may occur in ebbs and flows. There will be times when reflection and retrenchment come, especially as new challenges appear or there is a calamity. However, as the group moves along, finding more strength together for the work than they would apart, there is a noticeable shift in creativity and trust.

I once chaired a rather hostile meeting in a corporation that had asked me to lead an advisory group in one of its departments. On that day, the members of the committee were unfailingly polite to each other, but the tension in the room was palpable. I had been a chair for several months, so we all knew the ritual – opening check in and then working through the agenda. I did not know what was causing the hostility and had a sense that, as an outsider, I would not easily find out; this issue seemed personal to several of them.

We carried on with the usual ritual, checking off items on the agenda, starting with a focus question about what joys they brought with them today. The joys were negligible but the members of the group at least attempted to participate. Body stances told me who was angry with whom. While not an intentional liminal space, this meeting needed to become one, fast. So, I stopped the agenda ritual. I needed a new container. I asked what each person valued most about the organization and what she or he valued most about this particular department's work within it. With values on the table, we all could see where the conflict lay. I then asked them what they valued about each other. Body stances began to shift and ease, with one exception. The exception had polarized, and was deeply ingrained in the conflict, suspicious of any compliment paid him from others in the room. I left him alone at that moment because I needed to get everyone else back in the conversation. He didn't like it.

Once values and appreciation were on the table, we took a break. Little clusters of people gathered around coffee and snacks and talked with each other, including those who had formerly blocked each other with body stances. Relationship-building began again.

We reconvened. I asked about the issue that came into the room with them prior to the start of the meeting. A racism accusation had been flung out earlier in the day, and this group prided itself on its openness and attention to the "isms." The accusation had not been resolved and, in my role, I was not there to resolve it with them, but I did ask if they could talk it through among themselves after the meeting (transition their ways of being in relationship). They, with the one exception, seemed to think they could, including the injured party. We continued with the set agenda and closed with another round of naming joys. This time, everyone with one exception could name one.

This example does not describe *intentional* liminal space. Yet, it became liminal space for a short time so that people's worldviews and values could be put on the table. The meeting agenda was suspended and the situation called for conflict management where I held the container, asked questions that moved below the surface behavior and then let the group do its work. One chose not to participate and I did not have time to explore why. The rest allowed a disruption and created a new flow, signifying a desire to be in a different spot than where they found themselves when entering the room. The container loosened as the majority of the persons gathered found common purpose and willingness to do the work of self-examination to foster positive change.

Their flow went like this: they moved from their entrenchment, to uneasy transition, into promise of arrival in a new way of relating. If this group had desired to enter longer-term, intentional work in liminal space, then the container would have held ritual for deeper storytelling, naming fears, thinking about core inner values together, co-creating a future way of responding when disruptions occurred and focusing on generative conversation even when feelings were hurt and values were threatened.

The Third Way via Hope

The generative spirit that arises in liminal space that is facilitated well and fully participated in leads to new ideas and hopes. They rise into the air, like steam, and catch what they will, traveling where they are meant to go at the time. A new sense of adventure can capture a group at this point, as is often the case when generativity replaces entrenchment and self-protection. Flow and stance are met with creativity and energy. More deeply, a new sense of hope for the future emerges, with a vision for flourishing both personally and collectively. Hope narratives arise more frequently as the chaos of liminal space begins to settle into a new, more complex form. This is the time when the Third Way emerges most fully because vulnerability has been met with respect, stating one's own values is considered a sign of courage and the container holds people in their trust of each other.

The importance of hope cannot be underestimated. Creativity both generates hope and responds to it. I turn to theologians when discussing hope because there is a faith-aspect involved here, whether or not one considers oneself religious. Hope is not manufactured on its own; it draws from sources of imagination and belief that originate beyond our own feelings of personal optimism. German theologian Jürgen Moltmann describes hope this way:

> Hope is always a tense expectation and rouses the attentiveness of all our senses, so that we can grasp the chances for the things we hope for, wherever and whenever they present themselves. That distinguishes hope from mere expectation or patient waiting. When

all the senses are attentive, reason is the vehicle which conveys the knowledge of change. We then perceive things not just as they have become and now exist but also in the different ways they could be. We perceive things not only *sic stantibus* but also *sic fluentibus*, as fluid not static, and try to realize their potentialities for change in a positive direction.[3]

Moltmann continues his discussion of hope by attending to anxiety and fear as one stimulus for change. Fear, he says, sees the crises in place; it awakens our senses. The temptation arising from fear is alarmism, despair, or chronic anxiety that becomes immobile. On the other hand, hope sees the possibilities arising from crises. It too has temptation: utopian thinking. Hope, in its best form, takes fear and connects the present goals for change with future possibilities. Moltmann claims that resisting destructive tendencies in our world and anticipating powerful, positive change, calls us to move into the space where we encounter imagination and learn to anticipate what is possible and how we might move in that direction, in his framework, with faith and endurance.[4]

Another theologian, Croatian by birth, Miroslav Volf develops thoughts about flourishing in a globalizing world where religion and economics constantly interact with each other, either implicitly through assumptions about values or explicitly through political influence. His emphasis on flourishing contains within it a hope for the future that is based on a convincing kind of meaning-making narrative, focused on powerful, positive change on both a local and global scale. First, he identifies the problem:

Indeed, in the long development of global markets and communication networks, especially during the period of colonization, millions of human lives were damaged or sacrificed. Many ends achieved were and still remain salutary, but the processes themselves were oppressive and deadly. Today, too, while millions benefit from globalization, many suffer under it as well.

> Lives flourishing and love and lives languishing and despised – bread, water, and friendship given to the most vulnerable and these valuables withheld from them – would both have to figure in assessing globalization.[5]

Then he turns to the hope that arises from trouble:

> I believe that we should assess world historical processes in a way analogous to the way we should assess our own lives. Caught in the frenzy of living, we often forget what truly matters. Facing death, we sometimes get clarity. As there are no pockets in a burial shroud, what matters little to us when we are about to depart is not how much we have acquired, whether of material possession, fame, power, or experiences. Instead, what matters is how much we have loved and been loved in return, how much we have helped others to thrive and lead meaningful lives.[6]

For Volf, faith calls him into concern for his neighbor. For those for whom faith is not central, there remains a narrative in our lives that builds our belief systems; we each think and speak from our perspectives and never do so in a vacuum. To push further, when we craft a narrative that is self-focused based on personal success, we become restless, competitive and alone in the deepest sense. While optimism may surface in this state as an energy that continues our drive to get ahead, hope doesn't have a home here. Hope, by its nature, is relational, whether among human beings or among persons as they relate to history, the communal future, the state of the planet, the arts and sciences, technological interconnections or the intersections of stories held by others.

Hope narratives are essential for the future of organizations, relationships and personal thriving. They are a foundational part of what caregivers call resilience, a quality especially important when enduring suffering, living in long-term troubled times or encountering sudden disruption. Hope narratives also occur when energy is high and a diverse set of people find a synergy together based on common interest, cause or purpose, usually stemming from an immediate problem or crisis. The narrative is an imagination-based story that draws forth what we carry with us today and what we see as real possibility tomorrow. This story paints a picture of meaningful existence in our work and our relationships.

At its deepest level, the collective unconscious may reveal itself as this narrative of hope takes root. History shows us ongoing devastating crises and resilient response to them by the human race and the planet. In her book *A Paradise Built in Hell: The Extraordinary Communities that Arise in Disaster*, journalist Rebecca Solnit describes how, in numerous disasters from the 1906 San Francisco earthquake, to Hurricane Katrina, to 9/11 and others, citizens came together courageously and selflessly to demonstrate solidarity, altruism and creative improvisation, often in the face of resistance by authorities who wanted to disband them in order to assert control.

Thirty years after the 1906 San Francisco earthquake, a woman who was eight years old at the time of the quake recalls being in a large brass bed that rolled around the floor of the family's house in Oakland. She wrote this about her experience:

> What I remember most plainly about the earthquake was the human warmth and kindliness of everyone afterward. For days refugees poured out of burning San Francisco and camped in Idora Park and the race-track in Oakland. People came in their night clothes; there were new-born babies. Mother and all our neighbors were busy from morning to night cooking hot meals. They gave away every extra garment they possessed. They stripped themselves to the bone in giving, forgetful of the morrow. While the crisis lasted, people loved each other.[7]

And she remembers asking herself, at the age of eight, "Why can't we live this way all the time?"[8] That little girl was Dorothy Day. The earthquake was for her a spiritual awakening and the template for her life. After converting to Roman Catholicism, she founded the Catholic Worker Movement, treating poverty as the disaster in which she would create the sense of community, hospitality, and compassion she had experienced after the earthquake in San Francisco. The Catholic Worker Movement is still active today in more than 100 cities. When Pope Francis addressed Congress in 2015, he named Dorothy Day as one of four exemplary Americans, along with Abraham Lincoln, Martin Luther King, Jr and Thomas Merton.

Solnit's premise and Day's observation played out in 2020, when the world encountered the COVID-19 global pandemic, and again, people often came together even at personal risk to help those in need, providing shelter and food, entertainment for children during mass school-closures, comfort for the grieving, online socialization, and as appropriate, some relief for health workers who burned out or became ill from overwork and exposure.

Eons of response, for good or for ill, have been carried in our bodies and deeply influenced who we are today. Should we choose hope rather than avoidance or lethargy, we learn that disruption can guide us into liminal space, creating a place for positive change and deepening relational fields where powerful questions point us to a better future. History informs us, the present directs us, the future beckons us. The approaching horizon is close and the ideas are about to be set free through scenario-building and attention to emerging futures. The *status quo* is behind the team now and the stuckness is gone, with hope fueling an imagination for what's next.

Building Scenarios

As relational fields deepen in the team, family or organization, and as the container holds vulnerability that invites courage, in-between space seems less chaotic than the initial plunge into the threshold of change. Imagination and hope surface now and again until there is a sustained hope manifested as a sense of direction for the future; ideas emerge more quickly for a new equilibrium on the other side of the current liminal space. Like steam, dreams rise into the atmosphere and the team begins to think about dreams as potentials based on capabilities, resources and energy connected with purpose. Here, "what if" scenarios become the most powerful questions. At this point, the participants begin to find their common movement together; they can be aided greatly by a scenario-building process.

Building scenarios for the future is a craft developed for Shell Oil by Peter Schwartz, a global business network leader and entrepreneurial thinker, as long ago as the 1970s when the global oil crisis was just beginning. Schwartz helped Shell Oil to build scenarios based on what might happen should a natural resource shortage and a controlling conglomerate occur. When this crisis did occur, Shell was ready to follow one of the paths they had already imagined in response. Schwartz describes a scenario as a way to organize perceptions, both through imagination and discipline, about alternative future systems or environments in which decisions and goals might be played out.[9]

This approach to imagining the emerging future has been modified over fifty years, with versions still used in some business settings as a process to ascertain potential futures based on current events and trends in markets. The process can also be used for either personal or group foci regarding the future. This work is not an exact science, but makes examined probabilities part of anticipatory response, strangely enough, to the future. To do the precursor work for building scenarios requires keen attention to values, current events and trends and focus on purpose for the organization or group.[10] In short, scenario-building is a process that takes significant commitment and time to consider what might cause a problem, such as stuckness or crisis, followed by a well-thought-out response that incorporates both research and imagination. The hallmark of the process is keeping options open while observing what emerges, with possible paths forward already partially formed.

This approach to finding a different, positive way forward is not strategic planning with a pre-defined outcome that has a prescribed path to reach said outcome or predetermined mental arrangements. While there is organization to the scenario-building process combined with a sense of what is possible as it approaches from the horizon, the possibilities are loosely held until the emerging future becomes obvious. Multiple points of view are invited (attention to intersectionality is essential) and the inherent uncertainty found in liminal space is still in play.

Scenario-building begins when stuckness or crisis does not have ready response. Moltmann's reference to fear or a motivating level of anxiety may still exist. Certainly, there is a problem that draws the attention of the group or the leadership. As we know, to alleviate stuckness requires a willingness to walk into threshold space to let go of the routines and beliefs that are no longer helpful or relevant.

Liminal space within a container that creates purpose together is required for the team or group to commit to a meaningful scenario-building process, discuss findings, and then actively wait by observing and interpreting what falls into place as one or a combination of scenarios begins to play out. Then the path forward for the corporation or organization becomes much clearer. Scenario-building occurs in the creative space of imaginative narratives and rising stories about possibilities for the future and it also begins to draw together more concrete facets for informed choices about the path ahead.

This exercise, fully described in Schwartz's *The Art of the Long View* and in my own work with nonprofit and religious organizations, laid out in *Claiming New Life*, pays attention to the process of response to the unfolding future. In the past two decades, Schwartz's work has been expanded significantly via networks of business-based thinkers who have developed who have developed a link between past practices and emerging futures link past practices to emerging futures by claiming the imaginative narratives available to us in our present contexts.[11]

Creating space where generative work for the future can occur with parameters, but without given expected outcomes, is liminal space. I have discussed how this space affects individuals and groups desiring formational development but, clearly, these spaces, often called think-tanks, exist for the corporate world as well. Furthermore, these spaces exist in religious ritual, rites of passage in life-transitions and within groups of people hoping to better the future. Through liminal space, and discovery of one's own core values in connection with others' deeply held beliefs, relationships form that strengthen each and all, providing resilience for the future.

Positives and Negatives

Intentional liminal space can be entered for many reasons. Once immersed, people find various facets of flow in the space. Like steam, there comes a time when the work and relationship-development moves to a deeper level and begins to take on a life of its own, rising up beyond the original perspectives available when entering the space. This free flow can be tempered and harnessed by the purpose of the team, group, organization (or individual) as it (or she or he) explores possible futures, but also allows creativity to reach its best levels, generating possibilities that heretofore were unimagined. Such work is exciting work. The steam rises and intermingles with what it encounters. Likewise, the generative ideas and relationship-building move into a new facet of life, where a sane and creative leader or organization is loosed to be its best self, based in community.

However, there is also a significant danger which bears exploration. The threat comes when the excitement of a liminal, creative dynamic becomes one of two things: the participants want to stay forever in such a state because their own energy is pleasurable or the space becomes an addiction.

First, there are those who wish to stay in the generativity without attention to their own purposes and rooting in life. The generativity itself becomes the purpose rather than evolving into new equilibrium that exhibits a shift in life or work purpose and action. Put simply, there are those who spend their lives in conversation about possibility without ever taking action to make possibility real. They drift from idea to idea, thought to thought, with nothing resulting. Becoming stuck in liminality occurs when idea-mongers have no interest in the future but only in the rewards of the present, or by inattention to the movement or flow necessary to keep moving toward powerful, positive change. Motivation for this choice is often frozen fear or lethargy. The waters become dammed, trapped in an internal whirlpool or a stagnant pond.

Second, some people or organizational systems self-anesthetize, developing a pattern that looks and acts like addiction. Behavioral triggers and reactions remain unexamined. Following the path of least resistance to find temporary relief rules individuals or groups moment-by-moment. There may be unspoken or unresolved pain, fear of vulnerability, lack of courage or a desire to keep power isolated with little thought for relationship or connection. This form of captivity is isolating. The liminal space has been entered – not quite this (the past) and not quite that (the possible future) – and the desire is to stay numb. At its most severe, this addiction is defended through excuses and blame to the detriment of all involved. This stuckness creates a shame culture and is death-dealing, sometimes literally. Human health can decline and organizations begin to fade away, even if they have had significant past successes.

Bjørn Thomassen examines this state of immobility once one enters liminal space. He notes that spinning ideas forever is very present in whole societies, where people succumb to the propensity to create a carnival of life with the purpose of entertainment or risk-taking for thrill rather than meaning. He cites the entertainment industry as one example of this stuckness: "they display a systematic fixation on death and violence, sex and humour: universal limit or out-of-the-ordinary experience that have diffused 'kicks' must be seen as a search for constant excess and boundary transgression. . . . These kicks have no formative impact on the subject, so the craving remains."[12] Boredom leads to breaking boundaries through adventure for the sake of titillating experience more and more frequently, without a sense of genuine transformational change or connection to a large narrative. It fosters deeper and deeper meaninglessness and often depression, which in turn can lead to self-medication.

Thomassen's observations are echoed in Margaret Wheatley's claim that the decline of societies occurs when they enter the age of decadence, a petty and negative focus on consumerism, nihilism, fanaticism, imperial leadership, materialism, entitlements, narcissism and frivolity.[13] Liminal space, where people cross a threshold and keep desiring to cross thresholds without new equilibrium, grounded meaning or some connection with significance outside the self, can be dangerous indeed. It is important for those entering the change process in-between the past and future to do so with a team or another kind of companionship that facilitates healthy movement and powerful, positive questions for the sake of a better future.

Part III

LANDING IN THE FUTURE HERE AND NOW

The final section of journeying through liminal space includes a good landing in a new "home." This landing is transformed understanding of ourselves, the companions with whom we have journeyed and our roles in life. We have undergone a rite of passage of sorts, moving us from our old home to our new one, ultimately with change of focus and self-identity. In the midst of transitional time, we have had our worldview shaken, our pre-conceived notions of ourselves and others challenged and our creativity heightened. We have been pushed and supported. We have been listened to deeply and deeply listened to others. We have learned to be in uncharted waters without fighting the current.

What of this new home? We still have our obligations and our roles in day-to-day life. Our jobs require the same attention as before and the expectations of bosses, families and friends who have not shared our experience in liminal space remain the same. Yet we are different and there are some who might not welcome this change. The deepened sense of self and the heightened awareness of connection with others will not make sense to the world around us that has not undergone the journey through the in-between space and may even resist it.

The next chapter describes landing in the new home, the new way of being in the midst of these difficulties.

"Liminal landing"
Iceland, 2008

Chapter Seven

Landing

New Ground on the Other Side

Water, like religion and ideology, has the power to move millions of people. Since the very birth of human civilization, people have moved to settle close to it. People move when there is too little of it. People move when there is too much of it. People journey down it. People write, sing and dance about it. People fight over it. And all people, everywhere and every day, need it.
– Mikhail Gorbachev[1]

Having changed professions intentionally twice in my life, I have learned to traverse liminal space with some familiarity regarding my own patterns of pace through the waters and tolerance for risk while immersed in threshold. The range of emotion, challenge and sense of chaos that surfaces at various points in the journey is not comfortable but also is no longer alien. Transitions from one equilibrium to another included awareness-raising and then a long process, in my case, to mobilize myself to leave. The first time, I simply moved from a leadership position in a religious organization to a faculty position in an academic setting. The second time, I took a larger, riskier leap, moving from academia to create an independent small business based on my research and experience in leadership coaching and conflict management consulting. That transition lasted much longer than the first one because more chaos was in play regarding conditions for leaving the academy and learning how to create a start-up that attended to my interests and skill set, while also paying the bills.

Some nights I would look back at the shoreline I had left and ask myself, "What were you thinking? Steady paycheck and benefits, readily-available conversation partners as colleagues, classrooms in which to dialogue about ideas, all gone with no stable means of support or community to turn to!" Some nights I looked ahead as far as I could see, and said to myself, "Well done. Freedom tastes good. Things will unfold as they need to and doesn't it feel wonderful not to have to justify every thought or fill out reams of paperwork for someone else anymore?" In the liminal space, I had opportunity to go with the flow as I faced my fears, observed possibilities and began to believe more deeply in my own capabilities, took clear stances when people asked too much of me, and used imaginative narrative to free my dream so that I could begin moving toward its realization in some form. The new shoreline approaches.

I acknowledge that I have been privileged in the midst of intentional transition; I did experience disruption that started my leaving process but I had time to plan my transition. I had the economic support to re-tool and plan my way forward even when I didn't have a concrete guarantee of a future job. I had time to do my own scenario-building. Many people do not have access to such support, time and space. Nonetheless, it's a mistake to underestimate the tension and fear that accompanies the courage to take a large leap, no matter one's circumstance. At the same time, we know that these tensions and acts of courage are magnified greatly when people face sudden disruptions through tragedy, unexpected unemployment, global pandemic that strikes home, or natural disaster. In most situations, we look for the new equilibrium, the new landing as soon as we are able so that fear does not overtake us. It is often a luxury to be able to take time in liminality to build scenarios and expand one's outlook. However, if it is possible to do so, the intentionality of good travel through transition can make the new grounding more secure and stable, at least until the next disruption.

The journey through the flow of liminal space does indeed come to an end as we reach land again, for we human beings are primarily land-dwellers who create our homes on relatively stable surfaces. Liminal space is not meant to be permanent, so there is a natural closing phase as we emerge into a possibility-becoming-reality, or future-present. This is the moment van Gennep describes, when the boy who is of an age to engage a tribal ritual wherein he has been sent out to the wilderness for weeks to become a man turns his face to his village again. He has survived and he will be welcomed home as both a familiar and a new presence in his community. He sees his future unfolding. He will return and adopt his new role and his new place among his people, establishing a new equilibrium that carries his past, distant and immediate, and his future in the here and now.

Ultimately, one hopes that emergence from the liminal journey comes with expansion of belief systems, wider ways of knowing the world, deeper relationship, a sense of connection to the collective unconscious or ancestors, and commitment to, as Wheatley puts it, a sane way to be a leader in one's own community.[2] This new ground may be somewhat familiar, for the old ground has not disappeared. We have changed. We approach our lives, our projects or our teamwork differently, with renewed vigor and a continual learning stance. We have learned how to experiment and build imaginative narratives leading to scenario possibilities for the future. We have successfully coped with disruption. We have undergone the experience of the crucible, refining ourselves and our relationships, fine-tuning how we work and think. Our return to a new ground that allows for new equilibrium as we settle into the next phase of leadership readies us to encounter change within our new self-understanding and perspective.

What We Bring upon Arrival

We have been in the water or experiencing a facet of water for some time. We have learned a great deal in the flow and learned to trust our container. We have held our own (solid) and we have ebbed and flowed (liquid), traveled around corners, encountered hidden objects in ourselves and increased creativity and generativity (steam) as we learned not only to survive, but also to thrive in the company of others. The departure from our old ways of being or old worldview was painful in many ways. Grief may still linger. The new home, the new worldview, and, perhaps, responses, face us and we have the resilience and courage to live in new space as leaders who have changed.

There is a time of recovery and reflection that will help us as we emerge from the threshold waters of transition. We need to shake off the water without losing the experience of the flow. Liminal space does something to us and we would be well-served to write about, draw, compose or talk through what we have experienced. Our new home on dry land takes some getting used to and those who dwell in it will take some time getting used to us, if they are capable of doing so. The new home needs to be painted and decorated in our new style. We have landed and are making our new space habitable, shaking off the water and at the same time, always remembering the journey. Wheatley asks her most powerful question in the title of her most recent book, *Who Do We Choose to Be?*" To this, I would add one word: "Who do we choose to be *now*?"

Students who have any religious background at all often come to study in the liberal arts with stable notions of their faith constructs. If the academy adopts a continuous learning posture for its faculty as well as its students, it is likely that faith constructs are going to be disrupted. When students move through the curriculum to obtain their choice of degree in this type of academy, if they are open to learning, they find that their constructs are dismantled. This dismantling is unnerving if not downright frightening.

In my former theological seminary, I have heard I have heard hundreds of students claim that they feel adrift, that nothing makes sense anymore, that historical method and literature study have reduced all the "miracles" of their faith to explainable mythologies. Students react in various ways to this deconstruction.[3] Some entrench and claim that education is misguiding them and they transfer to schools that approach classical literature or sacred texts in a much more fundamental way. Others fight what they are learning or simply "put up with it" until they graduate and then revert to what they have always known. Students who can live through the deconstruction, with professors providing the container or the reassurance that there will be reconstruction and a new understanding in time, graduate with deeper faith and greater understanding of origins, contexts, and complexities found in their studies..

These new leaders are transformed; unfortunately, they move into a world that is unlikely to welcome their education and message either from a fundamentalist religious point of view or through a secular dismissal of all things dubbed religious. They find themselves stereotyped by the media who make uniform, unwarranted assumptions about religious leaders, often including unwarranted implication in any clergy scandals and presumed fundamentalist belief systems. Further, often they are not accepted by congregations or religious organizations that prefer simplicity with righteous certinalty over mature faith that engages life's uncertainties and plumbs the depth of human experience.

Yet, these transformed leaders cannot return to their old homes. They don't want to. They know too much. They have outgrown their space from the past. Their bubbles of belief have been burst and they have deepened their knowledge and reconstructed a more robust faith. Thus, they exist in their new homes and try to bring people along into the liminal space that they have experienced so that all might experience transformation. Sometimes their efforts are fruitful, sometimes there is too much resistance to change. Either way, the leader cannot return to the old home without denying the transformation that has occurred. The new home, the new worldview, begins to settle in, come what may. Who do they choose to be now? It depends on how they define their internal equilibrium and how much challenge they are capable of managing.

This narrative is not unique to the religious world. Education of any sort that teaches people how to think differently, more deeply and widely, about their own understanding, beliefs, or intersections in the world, evokes some level of disruption to equilibrium. Education, including continuing education and workshops, that teaches to the test or simply manufactures skill sets as measures of success is less likely to deepen and broaden people's lives. If there is no room for powerful questions and some level of disruption, then the *status quo* is maintained with an occasional incremental shift.

   This narrative also doesn't stop in the educational world. Organizational and family systems, while quite different in physical context, share a variety of behavior as human beings interact. This behavior may manifest differently depending on the setting, but it is unlikely to be turned off at the office, on the shop floor or at home. Organizations who reward obedience as the best form of loyalty are maintaining the *status quo*. Eventually, the leaders are enclosed in their bubble and the fast pace of change passes them by because they hear little in the way of meaningful input, including disruption in the form of critique. Learning organizations, as long-term thinkers Peter Senge and others have said repeatedly over the decades, are the most likely to be both quickly flexible and stable, holding the paradox in place at the same time. The same is true for family systems. The household that runs along rigid rules often experiences one side of a polarity or the other (or both) over time: complete passivity or complete rebellion. A learning household where vulnerability and courage interplay provides a better opportunity for maturing relationships and resilience when there is disruption.

Reflection on the Journey through Liminal Space

The journey through both calm and troubled waters will only make its deepest impact if the traveler spends some time in reflection throughout the journey but, most importantly, after arrival at the new shoreline. Particular questions arise about identity in the earliest immersion in liminal space and they may differ significantly at the closing of this space. For leaders, each question can take on a personal or a corporate note, depending on whether one is self-reflective or whether a group finds it useful to reflect together. The primary reflections are based on what one noticed (what was interesting?) and attended to (what mattered?) and how one mobilized for change (what happened?). Of course, the powerful question for the closing of threshold space is who do we choose to be now? Any number of questions may follow: how will we be together in that choice? What will we do with it and how will we get there? What do we want? A good facilitator will pursue these questions and be curious about how participants changed on the journey from beginning to end.

Other reflections can include conversations based on these questions or a version of them if relevant: What impact does this significant change make on one's own life and leadership, and on the life of others in relationship with me/us? What was most difficult on this journey? What was easy? How did the participant(s) change (water/steam) and how did she, he or they stay the same (ice)? What deep wisdoms and insights came from others in the group? What did I contribute? What do I hope for in the future?

Without reflection, the fullness of experience in liminal space will not be realized. Liminal space itself becomes part of life-experience. It provides us with a far more expansive view than our original home base, whether we are working on the future of a corporation's products and services or on personal self-identity. Reflection allows for the expansive view we learn in liminal space to be reinforced in ways that make sense for our context. Action-reflection learning is common in organizations and educational institutions that are interested in fostering movement in their work. Reflection at this point of moving into new equilibrium connects with feelings, dreams and analysis to provide a well-grounded landing.

Living Interstitially

The nature of encounters with liminal space is that we enter them and leave them, all being well, and then find our new state of being, our landing place. Our identity as leaders has expanded and perhaps resulted in changed worldviews, transformed roles and new paths in front of us for exploration or project implementation. We leave the waters of the journey into the unknown and land again on rooted ground, fortified with scenarios for the emerging future, ready for positive forays ahead.

This liminal immersion is not a one-time journey for individuals or organizational teams. As individuals, we live through phases of life, either demarcated by passages of age (the birthdays on the zero years) or via formal or informal rituals of maturing (first day of school, eighteenth birthday, twenty-first birthday, first job, first leaving home, reaching middle age, changing jobs, retiring and so on). We enter this kind of space many times. In most cases, society helps us mark the passage of time and think about meaning at each passage. However, our internal wisdom knows when changes are necessary and we may make big decisions at certain points in our family life or in our careers, depending on context, circumstance and energy level. Each time one of these passages occurs, we leave the "known" space and enter transitional or in-between space, to emerge eventually in our new home.

The same is true for organizational teams and corporations that continue to evolve. There are times when needs or markets shift and organizations pay attention. Or, they attempt to shift markets themselves because they are aware that nothing stays the same in the marketplace for long. Each time this shift happens, a leader and her or his team need to reassess what the organization offers and where it offers it, tending to capabilities and target customers or clients. Those who work in development offices or who influence the future of corporations or small businesses are well-served by spending quality time in the in-between space to sort out next steps, new products and how personnel will manage each. Organizations often express how pressed for time they are in a highly competitive, increasingly fast-paced market. The danger is that organizations themselves lose sight of their core foundations by trying to keep up with every trend. Creating intentional time for liminal work in a well-facilitated container will bring the leaders of an organization to a new shoreline with potential for a Third Way forward.

Religious and nonprofit organizations also often pay attention to changes in the world around them, though they are most often likely to be responding to problems rather than to initiating market change. Even so, these organizations cannot stay static and survive. This understanding of constant change necessitates immersion in liminal space to find the flow of creativity and meaningful work before their services and offerings can meet new needs, all without losing their core identity. If they do choose to disrupt systems that keep people in less-than-ideal conditions, then they have the opportunity to critique their own belief systems about their current work and the environment in which they do it.

In the midst of shock and grief, a great deal of blame is thrown around after a tragedy. Blaming deflects from the work needed, often immediately, to alleviate the effects of calamity. Accountability matters but the current reactivity seems to be entrenching polarities that are not being managed as public divide widens regarding, for example, slow responses to health crises such as coronavirus pandemic, or violence-on-the-rise blamed on lack of gun control. Sane reflection in a container that holds the conversation together might move us forward differently but only if people are willing to enter the liminal space of vulnerability and courage no matter their stances.

In each of these cases, we see the pattern of interstitial living. Interstitial in this case means that there will be multiple points throughout work and home life where disruptions occur and liminal space is entered, willingly or not. Put another way, to move forward effectively, one will discover that it is necessary to immerse in liminal space each time change is upon us, we wish to create change, or both. The pattern becomes much like Lewin's freeze, unfreeze, re-freeze, where we have a starting point, transitional in-between space and an ending point – over and over again. Lewin's linear approach is a bit simplistic, because we know that there is a great deal of activity in the "unfreeze" space, the liminality. We also know that liminality does not always unfold in a linear, straightforward, single-layered fashion. The length and complexity of each liminal space journey will vary as will the frequency of the interstitial points throughout time. However, understanding interstitial living allows individuals and groups to be less and less entrenched in the *status quo* or working hard to preserve it each time they encounter disruption. It also creates possibility for less resistance at the outset when people have an inkling what the flow might be like. Liminal space becomes welcome rather than threatening even if it can be a difficult space.

In centuries past, planned interstitial living occurred all the time. At particular points in the lifecycle, a ritual was performed to mark a formal change in identity. Van Gennep and others have pointed to social customs that marked rites of passages. Victor Turner studied rituals and their spiritual nature. However, as globalization renders more of society "generic" based on the consumption of goods and foods available worldwide, so too are the rites of passage becoming more recognizable, and perhaps generally less deeply meaningful wherever one locates in the world. Birthday celebrations and anniversaries are marked but a rite or a change no longer requires much input from the one celebrated or undergoing the change. Weddings differ according to religious custom in the world but there are some commonalities arising in vows and the meaning of colors and decorations. In many places, the culturally specific root of the liminal ritual has faded and the ceremony or celebration is simply customary, sometimes devoid of any deep purpose.

At the same time that purposeful ritual wanes in some traditions, in other realms intentional interstitial living calls us back to the making of meaning, creating a pattern of ritual that is its own liminal engagement, with great attentiveness to the nature of our roots and our rootedness. There is a countermovement afoot. A growing number of groups are attending to relational mindfulness and the collective unconscious as Spiritual But Not Religious movements rise around the planet. One example of this countermovement is called Nuns and Nones,[4] a movement that brings together women religious and millennials who are called "nones" because they claim no religion. The sisters in this movement take a prophetic stance to meet people in need through affordable housing, education, immigrant justice, climate resilience, gender and racial equity and more. They live together in shared community for spiritual practice and mutual work for the common good. The millennials seek to create lives of meaning through social action and spirituality, in community; they participate in these shared communities and adopt the values and spirituality therein as a central focus for their lives.

Many people attend regular rituals of their own making, sometimes based on what they may know of ancient rites of passage or rituals of renewal. Some gather at particular moon phases. Others immerse in the wilderness to find their deep selves. Still others practice rituals as a reminder of their own identity and are part of a long line of ancestors. Some redefine their religious traditions to create deeper meaning for their spiritual lives through small gatherings and variations of traditional rituals.

For now, in this interval of life, we have arrived in our new space. This new home itself can be dynamic and changing, but there will come a time when worldviews must be deepened and expanded again and liminal space calls or announces itself. We can enter with some sense of the flow ahead.

Positives and Negatives

Those who have entered liminal space, both intentionally and unintentionally, have to figure out a new way to live with others in relationship. Intentional space is meant to broaden a worldview while remaining rooted in that which sustains us. Unintentional space is usually filled with shock and loss and, most likely, fear. People here too must learn to live a new life, post-pandemic, earthquake, fire, death, war. The former liminality is gentler, with guided work and containers. The latter is harsh and, it is to be hoped, provides some kind of support in the midst of recovery. Either way, new relationships form and new ways of seeing the world arise.

In each case, grief will accompany change. With change comes gain but also loss. The old ways seem easier than reinventing ourselves. To make things even more difficult, people who have not journeyed with us tend to push back, wanting us to be predictable for them, as before. Families and friends may not like the new me or new you. Change-back messages are forceful and abundant: "You never used to be like this!", "What happened to you?", "Where is the person I used to know?", "I can't understand you now!", "You don't really believe that do you?", "How can you believe that?", "I can't take this nonsense!" and so forth.

Fortitude is required to sustain changed ways of thinking, creating, producing or, simply, living. Belief in one's self or in one's organization needs to hold steady and can with a support system in place. Sadly, and happily, this support system may end up being a new set of friends, new colleagues, new job or a new organization altogether. Our values and worldviews have grown and deepened and the old ways no longer work well. We have made our lives more complex but, ultimately, more fulfilling and meaningful as we move into our emerging future.

"The power of water"
Australia, 2018

Chapter Eight

THE NEW EQUILIBRIUM

Living for the Greater Good

The heart has its reasons, of which reason knows nothing.
– Blaise Pascal[1]

Journey's End, for Now

We have traversed the unknown into a new knowing. Each facet of the journey through liminal space adds a complexity of knowledge that leads to deeper wisdom, curiosity and a sense of adventure, perhaps with some tendrils of fear, about the future. Liminal learning is not linear, though it begins at the point of a threshold and ends on its other side. Within that in-between space, almost anything can happen. The importance of the container keeps a modicum of steadiness in the process of change. After landing and reflecting on our liminal journey, we now understand the process and what we have learned. If our learning has been deep, we have encountered wonderment, vulnerability and courage, a collective knowing, resilience and surprises. The heart and the head have spoken with each other and connected more deeply. Relationships have a closer connection even as greater differences have been revealed.

To be leaders who desire the world to seek health rather than destruction, we will need to invite others to move into liminal space, deepen commitments and relationships, learn trust, journey with the flow, generate scenarios and then return from the in-between space to do the work. This leadership focuses on how people in workplaces and families, friendships and collectives can live for the well-being of self, other and the planet. As Wheatley proposes, even if the majority of society is polarized, stuck in meaninglessness or attending only to self-serving devices, there will be enough "sanity" in small clusters that it can be networked. This network will provide a way forward that counters hate-mongering and planetary destruction in a sustainable, resilient way. However, creating these spaces focuses on the small scale, the local rather than the national or global level.

The genesis of a countermovement requires immersing in space that calls forth the best self. For the spiritual person, this call means integrating head, heart and spirit, denying the false dualism we have managed to construct since the age of science and the industrial revolution (head). Notions of love have become sentimentalized emotion through the marketplace (heart). Religion is becoming separated from spirituality as people tire of many religious groups' adjudication of rules rather than care for the soul (spirit). To be the best self, a person cannot live in separated compartments. To immerse fully in the flow of liminal space, all of these parts of our being are evoked as areas to be expanded and changed toward a greater, common good, starting personally and then connecting through relationship-building.

Businesses and nonprofit organizations may be reluctant to use spiritual language because of the secularization of society, laws of separation of church and state (in the US) that affect funded grants and the skepticism of individuals in the workplace. Some people do not believe in a spiritual self. Regardless, the integration of mind and heart remain on the table. Spirit is equally important for those who are convinced that spirit is a part of our humanness, animating us in ways that originate through an internal connection to a presence or force external to ourselves. Spirit may simply be inspiration for poetry and art or it can have more interactive communication. Indeed, those who attend to spirituality understand liminality innately, for they accept the mysterious (numinous) nature of the unexpected, which can arise at any time. However one defines the wholeness of personhood and community, the issue remains that our journey is to pursue emerging futures that help us learn to know what is yet unknown. The reason for this journey may be business success or a call to work for the greater good of the planet. It may stem from wanting the best for our children or a revival of cultural traditions in new contexts. The focus matters less than the quality of the journey and the choice about who we are as leaders and as human beings.

Positives and Negatives
CHALLENGES FOR THE FUTURE

Immersing in intentional liminal space challenges our dissociation from relationships, from organizational purpose and from our own rootedness. The contexts we face on the news or through personal experience, locally and globally, tend to shut us down. We attempt to create a safety zone where all the terrible things happening don't affect us. Ethnic and class conflict, dying ecosystems, decaying economies for the majority of the earth's population and disruptive environmental crises bombard us with messages of decline and doom every day; at some point, for our own sense of well-being, we have to respond. These responses differ and several serve to fuel the downward spiral.

One response is denial. Denial keeps us safe because we don't acknowledge the overwhelming messaging about destruction to our lives or we decide that all the messages, even research, are false propaganda that simply serves someone else's agenda. To be sure, there will be those in denial who see no point of the internal and relational teamwork in threshold space, for that would require transition work. Security and maintaining their present system, whether sustainable or not, is their primary concern.

Polarization is another response. Those who choose a stance without ability or desire to hear other narratives tend to know that there is problem (they are not in denial), but they need certainty about their own entrenched beliefs. It sounds like a version of this statement, usually embellished with a justification: "I have a clear belief and, if you don't share it, you are wrong." There is no compromise. The more people who are polarized feel challenged, the stronger their self-justification.

A third response is a compartmentalized compromise. This choice includes attempting to hear various perspectives but not embracing any stance in particular, allowing various influences to change one's opinions as seem attractive or prudent. Awareness levels about the state of the world are higher than those in denial, but the response is not consistently clear.

A fourth choice is general awareness and a desire to fix the dire news we all hear. Those who land here tend to be concerned about doing the right thing but may stop just short of being effective. They try to make the right decisions and take actions based on their belief systems but within relative safety; they worry about becoming engaged in conflict and are concerned about personal appropriateness and image.

Finally, a response that is rooted in a learning posture, which includes examined beliefs and is grounded in deep self-understanding, leads us to a more hopeful opportunity. A person who chooses this last response attempts to keep life balanced with gratitude and realism, while not succumbing to denial, chronic anxiety or despair about the state of the world.

All of these responses come from places in us that have been shaped by our environment, our own mental constructs and our belief systems. While some responses seem more helpful than others, there is no benefit in judging stances that are different than our own, if judging means that we dismiss them out of hand or dehumanize people who hold different beliefs. To do so leads to further denial, polarization, anger and anxiety. However, we can and must disagree with each other respectfully and challenge those who do harm. The state of the world is in great need of both sanity and a sense of hope.

HOPE

Thus far, we have considered rites of passage as customs in various cultures and societies marking change in identity, often prescribed by physical age or physical development rather than emotional and spiritual maturation. Understanding rites of passage as liminal spaces introduces this notion of "passage" or transition from one state to another. Rites are important to mark such journeys.

However, if we change the order of things, journeys themselves may create points where unofficial rites are important to mark endings and beginnings at different times and in different spaces. By intentionally embarking on the journey or jumping off the cliff anticipates and even invites liminal space as planned adventure rather than aa a response to disruption. The intentional liminal spaces in between what I have called the shorelines are where new or evolving formations develop and take root; change happens here in a contained way. Formation has its cycles of experience (or change cycles), in terms of behavior, and it also contains an arc or trajectory, an evolution, that carries some of the past with it but also is new. It is in this trajectory that we use imaginative narrative to co-create the arc-path forward. This path may lead to deconstruction as well as reconstruction of beliefs and values, plans and dreams, and habits and new ways of being.

Bill Plotkin, depth psychologist and founder of the Animas Valley Institute, understands very well the importance of liminal space for human development and maturation. His premise is that liminal space as nature itself invites us into deeper connection with our own depth of being, the ancient wisdoms and the intersections we have throughout the planet on natural levels.[2] He, like others, relies on archetypes as symbols for the collective unconscious and the ability of liminal space to call forth a formational process for human development. In the end, when each interstitial journey closes, our eyes are opened to new possibilities and to our new roles in co-creating the powerful arc for a holistic future. Those who function with a business mindset, Peter Senge, Otto Scharmer and colleagues, create liminal space through change theory based on the learning organization. Margaret Wheatley and Brené Brown capture the importance of liminal space as a place to develop courage of conviction, as well as compassionate stances with those people and acts that are destructive to human beings in business, community and society. Ultimately, intentional liminal spaces, with particular kinds of container in their midst, from nature to community hall to board room, are the learning spaces that foster powerful change for the common good.

As discussed earlier, unintentional liminal spaces, unavoidable difficulty or tragedy also have potential to evoke powerful responses, bringing out the worst or the best in people. When a loved one suddenly dies in an accident, the family gathers. Some members may be concerned about exactly how the memorial service will be conducted and what they will inherit, attempting to control everyone and everything so that they don't have to address or feel personal grief. Inevitable disagreements break out and others wonder how such family members can be so callous at a time like this. Some family members or professional caregivers may build a supportive container, showing kindness in the midst of grief, making meaningful connections with other members of the family and friends, going out of their way to conduct necessary tasks and care for problems, calming the chaos of disruption. They are the ones who invite the bereaved into compassionate space, which eventually helps the healing process begin. They are the ones who foster hope in the midst of difficulty.

How leaders build containers and how people live together in them, in all the facets of human intelligence and feeling, determines how we land on the other side of liminal space. The quality of the container directly relates to the depth and breadth of learning and change possible; in the healthiest containers, we attend to our core selves and the origin of our belief systems. Only when we immerse can we know ourselves at depth, thereby bringing our best thinking, our best work, our best presence to our places of influence for the sake of changing a small part of the world. In other words, we become the co-creating, proactive humanity we are meant to be on a planet that has desperate need for healthy connections.

As we journey together traversing the waters of the unknown future, we already are living in liminal space at a planetary level. We face peril as resources serving basic needs become strained for the majority of the population. The planet can no longer sustain all of us based on the way in which we live. However, there is hope created by movements of people who are investing in what they can do for the common good in their own areas of life. Leaders exist who know that, while they cannot fix this world, they can only be sane, as Wheatley puts it, where they work and where they live. I know enough leaders who do think this way; they act out of interest for others without denying who they are and what they need themselves. These leaders are familiar with liminal space, and they travel into the threshold between the *status quo* and the emerging future as they need to. These leaders are vulnerable and courageous. They have a sense of adventure and a sense of humor. They exhibit integrity and learning posture. Most of all, they make meaning of their leadership and invite others to build meaning for their own lives. They invent ways that bring forth a movement for powerful, positive change. Liminal space provides the transitional time and energy to move toward our emerging future, learning and living together on a path that brings new life and hope for the greater good.

"Liminality"
Australia, 2018

Epilogue

Liminality of Water

*When you put your hand in a flowing stream, you touch
the last that has gone before and the first of what is still to
come.*
– Leonardo da Vinci[1]

Water is the element that runs freely and cannot be tied down.
It favors running to the lowest places and fills any area that
will have it. Water holds and lets go. It heals and kills. There
is no defining water other than by explaining its chemical
makeup or by describing how it flows. There is no center to it,
no beginning and end on this earth; it simply circulates or is
held, sometimes for millions of years in one place. It exists in
sky, land and, of course, sea.

Jung's deep unconscious, the collective, is like underground
water, from whence the personal messages and the universal
archetypes arise. Our origins occurred in water, as did our
individual births.

Water flows everywhere, no matter how we try to control
it for our use or our safety. It is temporarily contained by the

borders of land through which it travels but it does not stay forever. Water is liminal unto itself. It is always in-between, always moving in some fashion, from point to point or from state to state. We are land-dwellers who immerse in water from time to time. Water flows on.

No wonder the ancient Celts understood so many of their sacred spaces in relation to water: wells, shorelines, tree groves near creeks or rivers. No wonder ceremonies of many religions include the use of water, for ritual cleansing or ritual encompassing into the life of a community. No wonder water is so powerful and gentle at the same time, a flowing paradox that can never be resolved but exists in tension.

Our lives ebb and flow like the tides. Whether we are attentive to them or not, we live our passages with liminal space. How much more healing, purifying, wise and transformed life might be if we do pay attention to the journey together:

> Water does not resist. Water flows. When you plunge your hand into it, all you feel is a caress. Water is not a solid wall, it will not stop you. But water always goes where it wants to go, and nothing in the end can stand against it. Water is patient. Dripping water wears away stone. Remember that, my child. Remember you are half water. If you can't go through an obstacle, go around it. Water does.[2]

Appendices

Appendix A

How Facilitators Create Containers in Liminal Space

Facilitators are people with effective skills in setting a stage, keeping focus, listening well, managing team or group emotions, holding containers where vulnerability and courage can be expressed and being accountable to agreed-upon timeframes. Organizations facing change are best served by contracting with an external facilitator to do the work described in this book. Bringing an external facilitator on board for a designated time period avoids internal conflicts of interest and provides room for as much objectivity as possible.

Here are components facilitators need to know before working with groups or teams immersing in liminal space.

In advance, the facilitator:

- Chooses participants or asks established leaders for participants who have the mindset and emotional intelligence for this work. The top leader(s) of the organization, division or department, depending on the team's scope of work, need to be fully present for the process.
- Needs to have a clear understanding of the work of the group – why is this group gathering and for what general purpose? Examples of purpose can include social change, spiritual formation, organizational development, dissatisfaction with the *status quo*, managing disruption, learning about a specific topic and/or creating new futures for nonprofit, for-profit or religious organizations.
- Needs to be able to coach rather than advise, soliciting deepening awareness through powerful questions without providing answers. The answers are already available to the participants; they simply have to find them. If asked for advice, the facilitator can provide observations or suggest resources or tell a story rather than telling the team or group what she or he thinks is best.
- Needs to have good personal boundaries and ethics regarding relationships and process. A healthy self-differentiation from occasional high-emotion or conflict in the space will be essential.
- Needs to have conflict management and/or group dynamic facilitation skills.
- Will need to know if she or he is facilitating a single team or group or is also facilitating a process throughout the organization if scenario-building is on the table. Clarity about role, timeline and expectations for the facilitator, via contract or job description, is necessary before any process begins.

In the process, the facilitator:

- Creates a container that describes this liminal time and space as having a clear starting and ending point.

- Describes the general role of the facilitator and occasionally, coach as and observer who keeps the container steady and ethical.
- Invites participants to name what is important for them in the team or group setting in terms of intercommunication, what is acceptable and unacceptable behavior (including use of language and levels of confidentiality) and what they expect from the facilitator within the facilitator's purview.
- Asks participants how they would like to open and close each meeting (a ritual, formal or informal, spiritual or secular). The ritual can include a welcome and a word from each person about a given topic or an answer to a particular question. It may include a symbol such as passing a symbol of the corporation, a logo, a candle or another object. A reading, quote or meditation can be included in the opening ritual to gather people in. The purpose is to create space that is familiar, steady and bracketed with ritual so that the unfamiliar, surprising, emotional risings in the team or group are held in defined space.
- Guides the process in the first gatherings, then steps back as the team or group learns to guide itself. The process includes a statement of purpose for the meeting, defines and keeps a clear end time, powerful questions throughout the designated time and then a summary of what the facilitator heard. Here, the facilitator asks what the group would like to discuss or reminds the team what they will be grappling with at the next meeting (setting the purpose), then moves to closing ritual.
- Guides the closing ritual as agreed upon by the group, which temporarily closes the container for that particular meeting. Closing may include feedback about learning (What did you learn today? What are you taking away with you?), feeling (What's going on in you right now?) and a statement of intention for how each individual is re-entering their contexts (Who are you going to be in the next two days?), based on what happened during the group members' time together.
- Offers appreciation for the specific work done and sends people forth.

Note: If this team is working in a collaborative organization, large business or corporate setting or educational institution and wishes to introduce scenario-building or different levels of employee buy-in to the process, the facilitator may accrue additional responsibilities. These responsibilities will need to be delineated and agreed upon before the whole process of facilitation begins with the original team. Responsibilities should not require gathering and analysis of data, feedback from groups or advice. Those tasks are the purview of the team.

Responsibilities for the facilitator may include:

- Inviting the original team or group to lay out a plan for communication with the wider organization based on a variation of the container space they themselves are experiencing. This plan will need to be clear about what communication means: informing, soliciting input, asking for observations as the process unfolds, etc.
- Training leaders for creating additional containers based on the communication plan. Checking in with leaders on a regular basis about the process and what might need to be revised or celebrated.
- Designating one person from the original team to accompany the facilitator when checking in with other container leaders, for the purpose of gathering feedback from other groups, as appropriate, to incorporate input to the team working on scenarios or ideas.

Appendix B

How to Participate in Liminal Space

Here are ways to be fully present in the immersion of liminal space for the purpose of navigating change well in times of uncertainty and transition. Participants may wish to read the role of the facilitator ahead of the gathering times.

Effective, engaged participants will need to:

- Respect the container and the expectations outlined for it, held by the facilitator and designed by the team itself.
- Understand that the facilitator is more coach than adviser. Successes and failures will be part of the process and the team will manage their impact. The facilitator asks powerful questions and manages conflict and emotions rather than purpose, data and emerging outcomes.

- Find a way as space and situation warrant to show vulnerability, courage and hold a stance respectfully. Be open to learning about where belief systems and values originate, rather than focusing on proving a point or winning an argument.
- Share ideas and concerns as they arise, in the container space rather than in the parking lot or at the water cooler.
- Attempt to live with temporary ambiguity for the sake of the process, even over a period of months, rather than rushing to find conclusions.
- Name ways to improve the container itself as the team moves forward.
- Participate fully for the whole process, especially in the midst of conflict should it arise.

Appendix C

A Summary of the Scenario-building Process[1]

The scenario-building opportunity for creating paths to engage an emerging future begins with preparation work, then follows seven steps. This process is best used with a group or organizational team already immersed in liminal space, after they have examined their beliefs, worked with discontent regarding the present system or realized the extent of disruption they face. It also can be used by individuals experiencing or choosing change on a personal or family level.

Preparation for the Work Itself

Preparation work can be modified or rearranged as is appropriate for each context. This work takes at least six months, though scenario-building groups can work concurrently after the team spends time addressing the first six steps. During this time, an external facilitator introduces the process. Then she or he travels with the team into this liminal work and renews or alters the container established at the onset of immersion into liminal space. This container allows for dialogue and critique within the parameters agreed upon by the group, which may have changed at this point in the immersion journey. Then she or he incorporates insights from the team into the wider organization by communicating the upcoming process, committing to updates and informing people where the team finds itself in the work. When these components are in place, the preparation of the team begins with the following powerful questions and subsequent conversations:

1. The facilitator invites the team to name the reality in which the organization finds itself, including the good, the bad and the ugly. What was going on that led to need or desire for change? What are the current circumstances?

2. The facilitator teaches skills for action-reflection learning by asking questions about the nature and purpose of the organization as the team understands it now, based on what they might imagine about the emerging future. This step initiates an ethic of inquiry and clarifies the belief systems and values that have been evolving in the change process.

3. The facilitator asks what beliefs and undergirding values the participants have discovered? How important are these beliefs and values to individuals? What has been underground and is now rising to the surface? What assumptions might still be affecting the conversation?

4. The facilitator invites the team to name what gives each persons energy in their work and in their lives. What increases this energy? What blocks it? What stories are available to tell about how this energy has evolved? How does work that brings satisfaction focus inward and/or outward?

5. The facilitator then explains the scenario-building process outlined below and is curious about how liminal

space has affected the team and how it might affect the entire organization as this change process moves forward without a named, preset outcome.

6. The facilitator invites ideas for creating a larger container or set of containers for the organization, either by teams or departments or at different levels. How might these containers be facilitated in terms of communication and regular employee observational feedback during the process?

Preparation for the Scenario-building Team

The facilitator explains the purpose and method for scenario-building, complete with timelines and expectations of team members, then asks for a consistent time commitment that is laid out over a period of six to eighteen months and invites the team members who are willing to name how they will hold themselves and each other accountable to the work.

Scenario-building

The facilitator initiates the process:

1. The team names the focal issue before the organization based on the preparation conversation above. A focal issue may be a problem, a disruption or an observation about standing still for too long in ever-changing markets.
2. The facilitator invites individuals or clusters of people to begin or obtain research about:
   - market movements;
   - movements in other organizations connected to their particular products or services;
   - international economic trends, short-term and long-term;
   - demographic changes or movements that directly relate to the organization;
   - observations about leadership learning trends;
   - the impact of marketing, messaging and attention to the common good on societies;

- observations about current politics, social issues and economics;
- generational preferences and behavior;
- news stories that make an impact on the community, nation or planet; and
- other relevant information that the team decides to pursue.

These topics will be analyzed and discussed by the entire team once the research phase is complete.

3. The team determines what external and internal forces lie behind the information they collect in Step 2. For example, demographic changes in the organization's area of influence may be due to immigration or emigration for a variety of socio-economic reasons (external) and ineffective or infrequent messaging may be affected by understaffed marketing division or department (internal). Determining *why* (underlying reason for the data) *and from what source* (within the organization's control or influence, or not) fleshes out deeper understanding of the research results in Step 2's categories. Step 3 is crucial for the scenario-building process and should take significant attention and time.

4. The full team ranks these forces in order of importance for the organization, giving particular attention to the top three or four. Then the team takes a break from each other for at least a week for each team member on her/ his own to develop three or four scenarios describing a potential future. These scenarios can be changed as many times as desired before bringing them back to the team. They do not have to be worst-case, best-case, middle-of-the-road case. They are meant to come from a well-informed (from the work above) imagination of the emerging future. This step is most likely to incorporate the head-heart connection, with some scenarios seeming very reasonable and incremental and others wildly exciting, with everything in between.

5. The team gathers and listens to scenarios. Scenarios are posted for all to review together. The team determines which ones address the original focal point and discards or modifies the others. This step is as crucial as Step 3. It loops back around to the focus of the organization, essential for fulfilling its purpose.

6. The facilitator helps the team decide which three scenarios are evoking the most energy and at the same time are within the realm of capability (even if a few organizational changes need to be made). These scenarios may be very different from each other.

7. The team connects with the leaders of the organization's wider container(s) and invites all participants to look at the scenarios and to observe which one or combinations of several seem to be unfolding in their department or division. This time of waiting and watching includes reporting back observations from all levels of the organization, with the team gathering the information at preset intervals for a period of four to six months, while the usual day-to-day work continues. A dominant scenario or combination of characteristics from two scenarios emerges and the new path opens.

8. Teams create increasingly detailed plans of action based on the emerging future; they are ready because they have thought through a variety of scenarios and so it is likely that unpleasant surprises are minimized. As the scenarios become plans and are implemented, a new equilibrium grounds the organization as it travels its modified or new path.

Benefits

The whole organization becomes a learning organization, each area with a sense of purpose and voice. The top levels of leadership hear from other areas of the hierarchy. Thus, they avoid an isolated bubble of assumptions and therefore are less likely to miss data, innovations and disruptions in the system of communication.

Liminal space fosters examination of relational fields, beliefs and values and self-awareness levels. It also leads across the threshold into a new way of being, a new role or a new identity – potentially for both individuals and whole organizations. It allows for conflict as a means of learning to be vulnerable and courageous, if the container is held well. Finally, it creates a deeper sense of connection to teammates and purpose in the world, with hopes for positively affecting the common good.

Endnotes

Prologue

[1] Leonardo da Vinci, https://www.goodreads.com/quotes/853419-in-time-and-with-water-everything-changes (accessed 10 December 2019).

[2] www.goodreads.com, tag "steam" (accessed 30 December 2019).

[3] I am indebted to John O'Donohue for awakening me to this observation in his book, *The Four Elements: Reflections on Nature* (London: Transworld Ireland, imprint of Random House, 2010) p. 43ff.

[4] Eila Kundrie Carrico, *The Other Side of the River: Stories of Women, Water and the World* (Cork, Republic of Ireland: Womancraft Publishing, 2015) (e-book) loc. 144-50.

[5] Sharon Paice Macleod, *Celtic Cosmology and the Otherworld: Mythic Origins, Sovereignty, and Liminality* (Jefferson, NC: McFarland & Co. Inc., 2018) pp. 216-17.

[6] Glenn C. Reynolds, "A Native American Water Ethic," in *Transactions*, Vol. 90 (2003) pp. 148-49.

[7] As differentiated from a polarity, which has the opposing "or" at each point. Polarity management embraces movement between opposite poles, while paradox holds both at the same time.

[8] I will use the terms "liminality" and "threshold space" interchangeably throughout this book.

[9] Adult bodies are composed of an average of 57-60 per cent water. See https://www.bing.com/search?q=how+much+of+your+body +is+ water&FORM=QSRE2 (accessed 10 December 2019).

[10] David Whyte, *River Flow: New and Selected Poems* (Langley, WA: Many Rivers Press, 2007).

Chapter One

[1] O'Donohue, *The Four Elements*, p. 71.

[2] VUCA is an acronym increasingly used in business and coaching discussions as a descriptor for the global, regional and local contexts in which organizations must function.

[3] https://www.dictionary.com/browse/liminal?s=t (accessed 2 February 2020).

[4] MacLeod, *Celtic Cosmology and the Otherworld*, p. 161.

[5] Arnold van Gennep, *The Rites of Passage*, English translation (Chicago, IL: University of Chicago Press, 1960) p. 11. (Original work published in French in 1909.)

[6] Ibid., p. vii.

[7] I am indebted to the Rev. Kristin Langstraat for sharing her workshop materials on ecotones as they relate to her workspace in the Ohio Health hospital system. See also "Ecotones and edges: Explaining abrupt changes in ecosystems," www.eco-intelligent. com/2016/12/15 (accessed 5 January 2020).

[8] Margaret Silf, *Sacred Spaces: Stations on a Celtic Way* (Brewster, MA: Paraclete Press, 2001) p. 12.

[9] Two clarifications need to be made about liminal space in light of the growing use of liminality to describe "not fitting in" to a particular group. First, while liminality includes a margin in terms of a boundary into or out of the threshold over which one crosses, it is not the same as marginalization. Marginalization can be permanent space on the "outside." Second, liminal space involves crossing borders, but is not equated with moving into frontiers. Frontiers are indeed unexamined places, but they do not necessarily have a landing or end point. In both these cases, liminality can enter the marginalized or frontier space, but there is a distinction between them.

[10] See Joshan Cooper Ramo, *The Seventh Sense: Power, Fortune, and Survival in the Age of Networks* (New York, NY: Little, Brown & Co., 2016) for an analysis of the networked world.

[11] See Parag Khanna, *Connectography: Mapping the Future of Global Civilization* (New York, NY: Random House, 2016) where he widens the technology discussion by asserting that world connectivity and devolution of political mega-powers in favor of urban autonomies is the emerging global future.

[12] Dave Gray, *Liminal Thinking: Create the Change You Want by Changing the Way You Think* (Brooklyn, NY: Two Waves Books, 2016) p. xiii.

[13] Ibid., p. 37.

[14] See Margaret J. Wheatley, *Who Do We Choose to Be? Facing Reality, Claiming Leadership, Restoring Sanity* (Oakland, CA: Berrett-Koehler Publishers, 2016).

[15] Ibid., pp. 6-7.

[16] Ibid., p. 10.

[17] See ibid., summary on back cover.

[18] One can delineate between "change" and "transition" here: change is situational and is often measured by outcomes. Transition is a process that starts with ending the current mode of operation or being and dealing with internal shifts to assimilate a shift.

[19] See William Bridges, "What is William Bridges' Transition Model?" http://wmbridges.com (accessed 6 January 2020).

[20] A clearness committee is a gathering by request of a person who needs to make a decision. The committee sits with the person contemplating change and listens, then asks powerful questions about what they notice in the conversation or in the person's non-verbal behavior. The premise is that the person has the answers already available internally and simply needs to bring them to the surface through this process. Gestalt coaching works much the same way, though with a more structured format.

[21] www.strategies-for-managing-change.com/kurt-lewin.html (accessed 6 January 2020).

[22] Gilbert R. Rendle, *Leading Change in the Congregation: Spiritual and Organizational Tools for Leaders* (Herndon, VA: Alban Institute, 1998) pp. 105ff.

[23] C. Otto Scharmer, *Theory U: Leading from the Future as It Emerges* (Oakland, CA: Berrett-Koehler Publishers, 2006). See also C. Otto Scharmer, *The Essentials of Theory U: Core Principles and Applications* (Oakland, CA: Berrett-Koehler Publishers, 2018) for a distilled and updated version of Theory U.

[24] Scharmer, *The Essentials of Theory U*, Dedication page.

[25] Ibid., p. ix.

[26] Ibid., p. xiii. The "container" concept will be discussed more thoroughly in Chapter Three.

[27] Brené Brown, *Dare to Lead: Brave Work. Tough Conversations. Whole Hearts.* (New York, NY: Random House, 2018) p. 12.

[28] Brené Brown, *Braving the Wilderness: The Quest for True Belonging and the Courage to Stand Alone* (New York, NY: Random House, 2017).

[29] Brown, *Braving the Wilderness*, p. 36.

Chapter Two

[1] Lao Tzu, *Tao Te Ching*, trans. D.C. Lau (New York, NY: Penguin Books, 1963).

[2] This work comes from my own Ph.D. project, in the Practical Theology Department: Women in Leadership Studies, University of Glasgow, 1993, entitled: *Moving toward Koinonia in the Church: Reconciliation through Group Work with Women*.

[3] Brown, *Dare to Lead*, p. 4.

[4] Wheatley, *Who Do We Choose to Be?*, p. 246.

[5] Ibid., p. 247.

[6] Ibid., p. 4.

[7] Anthony Stevens, *Jung: A Very Short Introduction* (Oxford: Oxford University Press, 1994) p. 47.

[8] Ibid.

[9] See Joseph Campbell's classic collected works in *The Hero with a Thousand Faces*, third edition (Novato, CA: New World Library, 2008). Note: This valuable collection, in its context of the early twentieth century, contains stereotypes of male and female development and roles. Since Campbell's original publication in 1949, Clarissa Pinkola Estés (*Women Who Run with the Wolves: Myths and Stories of the Wild Woman Archetype*) and Jean Shinola Bolen (*Goddesses in Everywoman: Powerful Archetypes in Women's Lives*) and students of Campbell have published numerous works that focus on women's perspectives by concentrating on the heroine as well as the hero.

[10] Stevens, *Jung*, p. 48.

[11] George Lucas credited Joseph Campbell's work as an influence in creating the *Star Wars* saga.

[12] Campbell, *The Hero with a Thousand Faces*, pp. 271ff.

[13] Joseph Jaworski, *Source: The Inner Path of Knowledge Creation* (San Francisco, CA: Berrett-Koehler Publishers, 2012) pp. 3-4, quoting Robert Jahn and Brenda Dunne, "Sensors, Filters, and the Source of Reality," in *The Pertinence of the Princeton Engineering Anomalies Research (PEAR) Laboratory to the Pursuit of Global Health*, special issue of *Explore: The Journal of Science and Healing* 3, no. 3 (May/June 2007) p. 326.

[14] Sandra Krebs Hirsh and Jane A.G. Kise, *Soul Types: Finding the Spiritual Path that Is Right for You* (New York, NY: Hyperion, 1998) pp. 3-4.

[15] Ibid., p. 7.

[16] John O'Donohue, *Eternal Echoes: Celtic Reflections on Our Yearning to Belong* (New York, NY: HarperCollins, 1999) p. xxi.

[17] Ongoing conversations with Blandy Taylor, sole proprietor of Acupuncture Advantage in Delaware, OH, 2009-19. Story told with permission.

[18] Dictionary.com (accessed 6 December 2019); Google defines "transformation" this way: "a thorough or dramatic change in form or appearance" (accessed 6 December 2019).

[19] Peter Senge, C. Otto Scharmer, Joseph Jaworski and Betty Sue Flowers, *Presence: Human Purpose and the Field of the Future* (New York, NY: Crown Business, 2004) pp. 13-14.

[20] See O'Donohue, *Eternal Echoes*, Ch. 3.

[21] Ongoing conversations with the Rev. Dr Sandra Selby, community minister, Akron, OH, 2007-19. Story told with permission.

Chapter Three

[1] Carrico, *The Other Side of the River*, loc. 176.

[2] Scharmer, *Theory U*, pp. 104-5.

[3] Gestalt Institute of Cleveland, Coach Certification Program materials, 2018, p. 14. See www.gestaltcleveland.org for more information.

[4] Amy C. Edmondson, *Teaming: How Organizations Learn, Innovate, and Compete in the Knowledge Economy* (San Francisco, CA: Jossey-Bass, 2012) pp. 125ff.

[5] Mary Pierce Brosmer, *Women Writing for (a) Change: A Guide for Creative Transformation* (Notre Dame, IN: Soren Books, 2009) p. 23.

[6] Ibid., p. 237.

[7] Ibid., pp. 182-83.

[8] Women Writing for (a) Change (WWf[a]C) circle led by the Rev. Dr Lisa Hess, fall 2017. Story told with permission.

[9] Gray, *Liminal Thinking*, p. 37.

[10] Brown, *Dare to Lead*, p. 98.

[11] Bjørn Thomassen, *Liminality and the Modern: Living Through the In-Between* (New York, NY: Routledge, 2014) p. 94.

[12] Rebecca Solnit, *A Paradise Built in Hell: The Extraordinary Communities that Arise in Disaster* (New York, NY: Viking Penguin, 2009) p. 153.

[13] Thomassen, p. 95.

[14] I acknowledge that some experts in the field of trauma therapy claim that ongoing storytelling about a deeply horrific event can

re-traumatize people, holding them in a state of perpetual trauma. Addressing disparate views about storytelling as an effective or harmful trauma response is beyond the scope of our discussion here.
[15] Conversations with the Rev. Jay Anderson in January 2008 and, subsequently, in 2010. Story told with permission.

Chapter Four

[1] Carrico, *The Other Side of the River*, loc. 182.
[2] Peter Senge, *The Fifth Discipline: The Art and Practice of the Learning Organization*, second edition (New York, NY: Currency/Doubleday, 2006). See also Chris Argyris, *Organizational Traps: Leadership, Culture, and Organizational Design*, first edition (Oxford: Oxford University Press, 2012).
[3] Gray, *Liminal Thinking*, pp. 13-19.
[4] Ibid., p. 19, p. 43.
[5] See www.mckinsey.com, overview, under About Us (accessed 21 January 2020).
[6] www.mckinsey.com/diversity (accessed 7 January 2020).
[7] Grace Reyes, "The ROI of Diversity: Delivering Business Success," www.forbes.com, posted 23 September 2019 (accessed 7 January 2020).
[8] See www.alliesforchange.org or www.melaniemorrison.net for more information about anti-oppression education and resourcing for those committed to social change.
[9] Arlie Russell Hochschild, *Strangers in Their Own Land: Anger and Mourning on the American Right* (New York, NY: The New Press, 2016) p. 5.
[10] "*Coach Certification Program Handbook*," Gestalt Certification Program 2018-2019 (Cleveland, OH: Gestalt Institute of Cleveland, 2018), pp. 69-72.]
[11] Laura Whitworth, Karen Kimsey-House, Henry Kimsey-House and Phillip Sandahl, *Co-Active Coaching: Changing Business, Transforming Lives*, fourth edition (Boston, MA: Nicholas Brealey Publishing, 2018) pp. 83-88.
[12] Wheatley, *Who Do We Choose to Be?*, p. 70.
[13] Karen P. Oliveto, *Together at the Table: Diversity without Division in the United Methodist Church* (Louisville, KY: Westminster John Knox Press, 2018) p. 55.

Chapter Five

[1] Ernest Shackleton quoted on quotlr.com (accessed 7 January 2020). Shackleton was an Antarctic explorer who was stranded with his

crew for over one year in Antarctica from January 1915 to August 1916. See Ernest Shackleton, *South: The Illustrated Story of Shackleton's Last Expedition: 1914-1917* (Minneapolis, MN: Quarto Publishing Group USA Inc., 2016).

2 "The Oldest Ice on Earth? Investigating buried glacier ice in the McMurdo Dry Valleys," Antarctic Research Project in *Ice Stories: Dispatches from Polar Scientists*, 2015, www.icestories.exploratorium. edu (accessed 7 January 2020).

3 See Margot Morrell and Stephanie Capparell, *Shackleton's Way: Leadership Lessons from the Great Antarctic Explorer* (New York, NY: Viking Penguin Books, 2001) for the full story of the voyage and leadership principles Shackleton used to save his stranded crew.

4 See Chapter Two for discussion of the collective unconscious.

5 The first hybrid automobile was built in 1898 by Ferdinand Porsche, though there are claims that the first electric engine was built in 1839 in Scotland by Robert Anderson. The first hybrid to go on sale on the mass market was in the United States: the Honda Insight in 1999. See www.autocar.co.uk and search for the electric and hybrid car's progress between the nineteenth and the twenty-first centuries (accessed 26 December 2019).

6 Hauke Engel, Patrick Hertzke and Giulia Siccardo, "Second-life EV batteries: The newest value pool in energy storage," McKinsey & Company, April 2019, www.mckinsey.com (accessed 26 December 2019).

7 The second of October 2019 marks the 150th anniversary of Gandhi's birth. "Mahatma" translates as "Great Soul." His lesser-known name was Mohandas Karamchand Gandhi. See https://www.mkgandhi.org/articles/gsouthafrica_satyagraha.htm for a description of Gandhi's protest on behalf of Indian populations in South Africa (accessed 2 February 2020).

8 Dennis Dalton (ed.), *Mahatma Gandhi: Selected Political Writings* (Indianapolis, IN: Hackett Publishing Co. Inc., 1996).

9 Robert E. Quinn, *Deep Change: Discovering the Leader Within* (San Francisco, CA: Jossey Bass Publishers, 1996) p. 196.

10 Ibid., p. 197.

11 Ibid., pp.201-4.

12 Brown, *Dare to Lead*, p. 271.

13 Dr. Toni C. King is associate professor of black studies and women's studies at Denison University in Granville, Ohio.

14 See Barry Johnson, *Polarity Management: Identifying and Managing Unsolvable Problems* (Amherst, MA: HRD Press, 2014).

15 ROYGBIV was the device we used in kindergarten to remember the order of the colors of the rainbow from hot to cold: red, orange,

156   Leadership in Unknown Waters

yellow, green, blue, indigo, violet. We were enamored with rainbows because they displayed these colors in this order. Later in school the study of refraction explained how rainbows occurred.

[16] Bim Adewunmi, "Kimberlé Crenshaw on Intersectionality: 'I wanted to come up with an everyday metaphor that anyone could use'," *New Statesman*, 2 April 2014, www.newstatesman.com (accessed 26 December 2019).

[17] There is a large body of writing by Jung and subsequent literature in the field of Jungian psychology, which has evolved and expanded. For a brief overview of Jung's development of psychological theory and its contrasts with Freudian psychology, see, again, Stevens, *Jung*.

[18] Ibid., p. 47.

[19] There are myriad resources describing archetypes for life-journeys, leadership and ritual passages from youth to adulthood; this is beyond the scope of the discussion here.

[20] Stevens, *Jung*, p. 48.

[21] Jung's theory was hotly contested in his day by psychologists who insisted that newborns were blank slates, with their behavior developing through experienced stimuli. Jung countered that experienced stimuli create uniqueness; even in the non-human world, a chick knows how to make its way out of the egg, geese know how to navigate to their summer and winter homes and a bird knows how to build a nest without being taught.

Chapter Six

[1] Goodreads.com, tag "steam" (accessed 30 December 2019).

[2] I have led groups like this for over 30 years, sometimes for spiritual formation and other times to generate ideas or scenarios for the future of organizations. This particular group was comprised of women who attended a church but were dissatisfied with the level of learning and formation available there. They were much like the current Spiritual But Not Religious (SBNR) group, with the subcategory "Dones" – disenfranchised by church – studied by sociologists today.

[3] Jürgen Moltmann, *Ethics of Hope* (Minneapolis, MN: Fortress Press, 2012) p. 3.

[4] Ibid., pp. 3-8.

[5] Miroslav Volf, *Flourishing: Why We Need Religion in a Globalized World* (New Haven, CT: Yale University Press, 2015) p. 16.

[6] Ibid.

[7] Solnit, *A Paradise Built in Hell*, pp. 59-60.

[8] Rebecca Solnit, "Falling Together," On Being with Krista Tippett, 26 May 2016, transcript of interview, p. 6, https://www.onbeing.org.

[9] Peter Schwartz, *The Art of the Long View: Planning for the Future in an Uncertain World* (New York, NY: Currency, 1991) p. 4.

[10] I discuss scenario-building as a seven-step process in detail with several examples in an earlier book, *Claiming New Life* (St Louis, MO: Chalice Press, 2008). See Appendix C for a short list describing the process.

[11] See the Presencing Institute at Massachusetts Institute of Technology (www.presencing.org) and the Society for Organizational Learning (www.solonline.org); see also Scharmer, *Theory U*; Senge, Scharmer, Jaworski and Flowers, *Presence*; and Jaworski, *Source*.

[12] Thomassen, *Liminality and the Modern*, p. 189.

[13] Wheatley, *Who Do We Choose to Be?*, p. 36.

Chapter Seven

[1] See www.azquotes.com/authors/m/Mikhail Gorbachev (accessed 1 January 2020).

[2] Wheatley, *Who Do We Choose to Be?*, summary on back cover.

[3] Ironically, seminary students who have little or no religious background do not experience deconstruction and are more open to learning what normally might be disruptive worldviews. Often, they do not intend to enter leadership in religious organizations; rather, they are interested in spiritual formation and religious history as informative for their career paths in mostly nonprofit organizations or entrepreneurial endeavors, especially relating to ecology, economic justice and caregiving in non-traditional settings such as prisons, mental health institutions, with people living on the margins, in hospital emergency departments, etc.

[4] See www.nunsandnones.org (accessed 30 December 2019).

Chapter Eight

[1] www.goodreads.com, tag "Pascal" (accessed 30 December 2019).

[2] See Bill Plotkin, *Nature and the Human Soul: Cultivating Wholeness and Community in a Fragmented World* (Novato, CA: New World Library, 2008) for a thorough discussion of the personal and cultural transformation possible should we choose a sustainable, collaborative and compassionate path forward in our world. He attends to archetypes, spirituality, development theory and liminal space of the natural world in his challenge for change.

Epilogue

[1] Leonardo da Vinci, https://www.azquotes.com/quotes/topics/water.html (accessed 30 December 2019).
[2] Margaret Atwood, *The Penelopiad: The Myth of Penelope and Odysseus* (Edinburgh: Canongate Books Ltd, 2005).

Appendix C

[1] Adapted originally from Schwartz, *The Art of the Long View*, and, recently, from Withrow, *Claiming New Life*.

Bibliography

Books and E-books

Argyris, Chris, *Organizational Traps: Leadership, Culture, and Organizational Design*, first edition (Oxford: Oxford University Press, 2012)

Atwood, Margaret, *The Penelopiad: The Myth of Penelope and Odysseus* (Edinburgh: Canongate Books Ltd, 2005)

Bolen, Jean Shinoda, *Goddesses in Everywoman: Powerful Archetypes in Women's Lives*, first edition (New York, NY: Harper & Row Publishers Inc., 1984)

Brosmer, Mary Pierce, *Women Writing for (a) Change: A Guide for Creative Transformation* (Notre Dame, IN: Soren Books, 2009)

Brown, Brené, *Braving the Wilderness: The Quest for True Belonging and the Courage to Stand Alone* (New York, NY: Random House, 2017)

———, *Dare to Lead: Brave Work. Tough Conversations. Whole Hearts.* (New York, NY: Random House, 2018)

Campbell, Joseph, *The Hero with a Thousand Faces*, third edition (Novato, CA: New World Library, 2008)

Carrico, Eila Kundrie, *The Other Side of the River: Stories of Women, Water and the World* (Cork, Republic of Ireland: Womancraft Publishing, 2015) (e-book)

Dalton, Dennis (ed.), *Mahatma Gandhi: Selected Political Writings* (Indianapolis, IN: Hackett Publishing Co. Inc., 1996)

Edmondson, Amy C., *Teaming: How Organizations Learn, Innovate, and Compete in the Knowledge Economy* (San Francisco, CA: Jossey-Bass, 2012)

Estés, Clarissa Pinkola, *Women Who Run with the Wolves: Myths and Stories of the Wild Woman Archetype* (New York, NY: Ballantine Books, 1992)

Gennep, Arnold van, *The Rites of Passage*, English translation (Chicago, IL: University of Chicago Press, 1960) (Original work published in French in 1909)

Gray, Dave, *Liminal Thinking: Create the Change You Want by Changing the Way You Think* (Brooklyn, NY: Two Waves Books, 2016)

Hirsh, Sandra Krebs, and Jane A.G. Kise, *Soul Types: Finding the Spiritual Path that Is Right for You* (New York, NY: Hyperion, 1998)

Hochschild, Arlie Russell, *Strangers in Their Own Land: Anger and Mourning on the American Right* (New York, NY: The New Press, 2016)

Jahn, Robert, and Brenda Dunne, "Sensors, Filters, and the Source of Reality," in *The Pertinence of the Princeton Engineering Anomalies Research (PEAR) Laboratory to the Pursuit of Global Health*, special issue of *Explore: The Journal of Science and Healing* 3, no. 3 (May/June 2007)

Jaworski, Joseph, *Source: The Inner Path of Knowledge Creation* (San Francisco, CA: Berrett-Koehler Publishers Inc., 2012)

Johnson, Barry, *Polarity Management: Identifying and Managing Unsolvable Problems* (Amherst, MA: HRD Press, 2014)

Khanna, Parag, *Connectography: Mapping the Future of Global Civilization* (New York, NY: Random House, 2016)

Lao Tzu, *Tao Te Ching*, trans. D.C. Lau (New York, NY: Penguin Putnam Inc., 1963)

Macleod, Sharon Paice, *Celtic Cosmology and the Otherworld: Mythic Origins, Sovereignty, and Liminality* (Jefferson, NC: McFarland & Co. Inc., 2018)

Moltmann, Jürgen, *Ethics of Hope* (Minneapolis, MN: Fortress Press, 2012)

Morrell, Margot, and Stephanie Capparell, *Shackleton's Way: Leadership Lessons from the Great Antarctic Explorer* (New York, NY: Viking Penguin Books, 2001)

O'Donohue, John, *Eternal Echoes: Celtic Reflections on Our Yearning to Belong* (New York, NY: HarperCollins, 1999)

— — —, *The Four Elements: Reflections on Nature* (London: Transworld Ireland, imprint of Random House, 2010)

Oliveto, Karen P., *Together at the Table: Diversity without Division in the United Methodist Church* (Louisville, KY: Westminster John Knox Press, 2018)

Plotkin, Bill, *Nature and the Human Soul: Cultivating Wholeness and Community in a Fragmented World* (Novato, CA: New World Library, 2008)

Quinn, Robert E., *Deep Change: Discovering the Leader Within* (San Francisco, CA: Jossey Bass Publishers, 1996)

Ramo, Joshan Cooper, *The Seventh Sense: Power, Fortune, and Survival in the Age of Networks* (New York, NY: Little, Brown & Co., 2016)

Rendle, Gilbert R., *Leading Change in the Congregation: Spiritual and Organizational Tools for Leaders* (Herndon, VA: Alban Institute, 1998)

Reynolds, Glenn C., "A Native American Water Ethic," in *Transactions*, Vol. 90 (2003)

Scharmer, C. Otto, *Theory U: Leading from the Future as It Emerges* (Oakland, CA: Berrett-Koehler Publishers, 2006)

— — —, *The Essentials of Theory U: Core Principles and Applications* (Oakland, CA: Berrett-Koehler Publishers, 2018)

Schwartz, Peter, *The Art of the Long View: Planning for the Future in an Uncertain World* (New York, NY: Currency, 1991)

Senge, Peter, *The Fifth Discipline: The Art and Practice of the Learning Organization*, second edition (New York, NY: Currency/Doubleday, 2006)

Senge, Peter, C. Otto Scharmer, Joseph Jaworski and Betty Sue Flowers, *Presence: Human Purpose and the Field of the Future* (New York, NY: Crown Business, 2004)

Shackleton, Ernest, *South: The Illustrated Story of Shackleton's Last Expedition: 1914-1917* (Minneapolis, MN: Quarto Publishing Group USA Inc., 2016)

Silf, Margaret, *Sacred Spaces: Stations on a Celtic Way* (Brewster, MA: Paraclete Press, 2001)

Solnit, Rebecca, *A Paradise Built in Hell: The Extraordinary Communities that Arise in Disaster* (New York, NY: Viking Penguin, 2009)

Stevens, Anthony, *Jung: A Very Short Introduction* (Oxford: Oxford University Press, 1994)

Thomassen, Bjørn, *Liminality and the Modern: Living Through the In-Between* (New York, NY: Routledge, 2014)

Volf, Miroslav, *Flourishing: Why We Need Religion in a Globalized World* (New Haven, CT: Yale University Press, 2015)

Wheatley, Margaret J., *Who Do We Choose to Be? Facing Reality, Claiming Leadership, Restoring Sanity* (Oakland, CA: Berrett-Koehler Publishers, 2017)

Whitworth, Laura, Karen Kimsey-House, Henry Kimsey-House and Phillip Sandahl, *Co-Active Coaching: Changing Business, Transforming Lives*, fourth edition (Boston, MA: Nicholas Brealey Publishing, 2018)

Whyte, David, *River Flow: New and Selected Poems* (Langley, WA: Many Rivers Press, 2007)

Withrow, Lisa R., *Claiming New Life* (St Louis, MO: Chalice Press, 2008)

———, *Moving toward Koinonia in the Church: Reconciliation through Group Work with Women*. Ph.D. project, University of Glasgow, 1993, unpublished

Websites
(By Author)

Adewunmi, Bim, "Kimberlé Crenshaw on Intersectionality: 'I wanted to come up with an everyday metaphor that anyone could use'," *New Statesman*, 2 April 2014, http://newstatesman.com

Bridges, William, "What is William Bridges' Transition Model?" http://wmbridges.com

Engel, Hauke, Patrick Hertzke and Giulia Siccardo, "Second-life EV batteries: The newest value pool in energy storage," McKinsey & Company, April 2019, http://www.mckinsey.com

Reyes, Grace, "The ROI of Diversity: Delivering Business Success," Forbes council post, www.forbes.com, 23 September 2019

Solnit, Rebecca, "Falling Together," On Being with Krista Tippett, 26 May 2016, transcript of interview, https://www.onbeing.org

(By Subject)

Diversity: www.mckinsey.com; www.alliesforchange.org; www.melaniemorrison.net

Ecotones: "Ecotones and edges: Explaining abrupt changes in ecosystems," www.eco-intelligent.com/2016/12/15

Electric and hybrid automobiles: www.autocar.co.uk, search history of hybrid and electric cars

Gestalt Institute of Cleveland: www.gestaltcleveland.org

Ice: "The Oldest Ice on Earth? Investigating buried glacier ice in the McMurdo Dry Valleys," Antarctic Research Project in *Ice Stories: Dispatches from Polar Scientists*, 2015, www.icestories.exploratorium.edu

Kurt Lewin and managing change: www.strategies-for-managing-change.com/kurt-lewin.html

Learning Organizations:

Presencing Institute at MIT: http://www.presencing.org

Society for Organizational Learning: http://www.solonline.org

Nuns and Nones: www.nunsandnones.org

Women Writing for (a) Change: www.womenwriting.org

Index

ON THE SAME SUBJECT:

Crossing Thresholds
A Practical Theology of Liminality
in Christian Discipleship, Worship and Mission

By Nigel Rooms, Timothy Carson,
Lisa R. Withrow, Rosemary Fairhurst

A comprehensive and systematic collection of essays dealing with the concept of liminality from a theological standpoint.

Specifications: 234x156mm (9.21x6.14in) / Forthcoming January 2021
Paperback ISBN: 978 0 7188 9346 0 / ePub ISBN: 978 0 7188 4239 0
PDF ISBN: 978 0 7188 4237 6

Neither Here nor There
The Many Voices of Liminality

Edited by Timothy Carson

An interdisciplinary anthology of essays exploring the concept of liminality and its fruitful application across a wide range of contemporary subjects.

Specifications: 234x156mm (9.21x6.14in), 270pp / Published: February 2019
Paperback ISBN: 978 0 7188 9543 3 / ePub ISBN: 978 0 7188 4788 3
Kindle ISBN: 978 0 7188 4789 0 / PDF ISBN: 978 0 7188 4787 6

Liminal Reality and Transformational Power
Revised Edition: Transition, Renewal and Hope

By Timothy Carson

An important study of the varieties of liminality, illuminating in particular the liminal aspects of pastoral leadership.

Specifications: 234x156mm (9.21x6.14in), 110pp / Published: April 2016
Paperback ISBN: 978 0 7188 9401 6 / ePub ISBN: 978 0 7188 4401 1
Kindle ISBN: 978 0 7188 4402 8 / PDF ISBN: 978 0 7188 4400 4